BrightRED Results

Credit
MATHS

J K Wilson

First published in 2009 by:

Bright Red Publishing Ltd
6 Stafford Street
Edinburgh
EH3 7AU

With thanks to PDQ (layout) and Ivor Normand (copy-edit)

Cover design by Caleb Rutherford – eidetic

Illustrations by PDQ Digital Media Solutions

Acknowledgements

Every effort has been made to seek all copyright holders. If any have been overlooked then Bright Red Publishing will be delighted to make the necessary arrangements.

Bright Red Publishing would like to thank the Scottish Qualifications Authority for use of Past Exam Questions. Answers do not emanate from SQA.

Contents

Introduction

How Does This Book Work

This book is to help prepare you for the Standard Grade Mathematics Credit exam by breaking down exam style questions. The solution to each question has comments running side by side explaining the thought process involved in each line of working. Although the solution is individual to each example, you should be able to apply the process to similar questions.

The book groups topics into 5 categories: Arithmetic, Algebra, Geometry, Trigonometry and Statistics. A recap of each topic is given before any examples are attempted. However, this book is not meant to teach the credit course. Instead, it should be used in conjunction with the information you have learnt in school to help you prepare you for the exam.

The only way to get good at Mathematics is to practice it. Reading this book and your notes is not enough to prepare you for the exam. It's very easy to understand what to do when you are reading and following a solution. You may find it useful to try and answer each example on your own and then compare your solution with the one in the book. Ultimately you want to be able to use the skills you have developed to answer past exam papers.

The Exam

The Credit Mathematics exam is split into 2 papers: Non-Calculator (Paper I) and Calculator (Paper II). Paper I is 45 minutes long and Paper II is 1 hour 20 minutes.

Each paper contains questions examining Knowledge and Understanding (KU) and Reasoning and Enquiry (RE). This book contains examples of both types of questions.

As you have no doubt been told endless times by your teacher "You must show your working!" This is a very important point as you may not get all the marks available for a question if you do not support it with appropriate working – even if the final answer is correct. This book shows you how to set out your working to allow you to get as many marks available as possible. (The number of lines of working in the solutions does not directly correspond to the number of marks a question would be worth).

The credit exam has a formulae sheet at the front of the paper. Make sure you are aware of the formulae on it. If there are a few formulae that you struggle to remember, write them onto the formulae sheet as soon as you are told you can start writing. Then they are there for when you need them.

Calculator

You must use at least a Scientific Calculator for the Credit Paper II exam. It is helpful if you have bought your own calculator before the exam so that you are familiar with how to work it.

And Finally ...

If you get stuck when you're revising then ask your teacher for help. They will be delighted that you are keen to do well and are spending time revising. If your school offers after school revision classes/ supported study then you might find it useful to attend.

Be confident in your own ability. If you're not sure how to answer a question trust your instincts and just give it a go anyway.

Good luck!

Order of Operations and Fractions

You should know the order in which to carry out calculations.

The BODMAS memory aid at the side can help you to remember it.

Brackets
Of
Divide
Multiply
Add
Subtract

Example

Evaluate $9 \cdot 54 - 1 \cdot 7 \times 4$

Solution

$$\begin{array}{r} 1 \cdot 7 \\ \times 4 \\ \hline 6 \cdot 8 \end{array}$$

▶ Work out the multiplication first – setting it out like this should make it easier.

$$\begin{array}{r} 9 \cdot 54 \\ -\ 6 \cdot 80 \\ \hline 2 \cdot 74 \end{array}$$

▶ Set your subtraction out like this to make sure you get the correct answer.

Look out for

'Of' means 'multiply'.

Example

$$\frac{3}{4}\left(2\frac{1}{3}+1\frac{5}{6}\right)$$

Solution

$$\frac{3}{4}\left(2\frac{2}{6}+1\frac{5}{6}\right)$$ ▶ Work out the bracket first by finding a common denominator.

$$=\frac{3}{4}\left(3\frac{7}{6}\right)$$ ▶ Change the mixed number into a top-heavy fraction.

$$=\frac{3}{4}\times 4\frac{1}{6}$$

$$=\frac{3}{4}\times\frac{25}{6}$$

$$=\frac{1}{4}\times\frac{25}{2}$$ ▶ Simplifying before you multiply makes the multiplication easier.

$$=\frac{25}{8}$$ ▶ Check that your answer is in its simplest form. You don't need to give your answer as a mixed number, but you can if you want

$$\left(=3\frac{1}{8}\right)$$

Example

$$1\frac{1}{8}+\frac{3}{4}\text{ of }2\frac{1}{3}$$

Solution

$$=1\frac{1}{8}+\left[\frac{3}{4}\times 2\frac{1}{3}\right]$$ ▶ You need to do the multiplication part first (think of BODMAS). This can be separated off by putting it in a bracket to make it easier.

$$=1\frac{1}{8}+\left[\frac{3}{4}\times\frac{7}{3}\right]$$ ▶ Change what's inside the bracket to a top-heavy fraction.
▶ Simplify the fractions where possible before multiplying.

$$=1\frac{1}{8}+\frac{7}{4}$$ ▶ Evaluate the bracket.

$$=1\frac{1}{8}+\frac{14}{8}$$ ▶ Add your fractions – check for a common denominator first!

$$=1\frac{15}{8}$$

$$=2\frac{7}{8}$$ ▶ Fully simplify your answer.

Interest

Simple Interest

Simple interest is interest paid only on the initial amount of money and not on previous interest earned. Questions on simple interest tend to appear in the General Mathematics paper.

For example, Paul pays £1500 into a savings account. Simple interest is paid at 4·2% per annum. If Paul does not withdraw any money from the account, what will his balance be after seven months?

$$4·2\% \text{ of } £1500 = 0·042 \times 1500$$
$$= £63$$

Interest for 1 year = £63

Interest for 7 months = £63 ÷ 12 × 7
$$= £36·75$$

Balance after 7 months = £1500 + £36·75 = £1536·75

Look out for

Per annum (p.a.) means each year.

Compound Interest

Compound interest is interest paid on the full balance of the account, including any previous interest earned.

For example, Paul pays £1500 into a savings account. Compound interest is paid at 4·2% per annum. If Paul does not withdraw any money from the account, what will his balance be after 3 years?

104·2% of £1500 = 1·042 × £1500 = £1563
104·2% of £1563 = 1·042 × £1563 = £1628·65
104·2% of £1628·65 = 1·042 × £1628·65 = £1697·05

A quicker way to work out compound interest is to make one calculation.
Taking the example above, we have actually found: 1·042 × 1·042 × 1·042 × £1500 = £1697·05

Or, in an even simpler format: $1·042^3 \times £1500 = £1697·05$

This method will always work when the percentage remains the same over a given period of time. The length of time will always be the power of the percentage. (This method will also help you with the Recurrence Relations chapter if you choose to go on and study Higher Mathematics.)

Appreciation and Percentage Increase

When the value of an item increases over a period of time, it's said to appreciate.

Example

The value of a house in 2007 was £129 000. The value of the house appreciates by 12% per annum.

What will the value of the house be in 2010?

Solution

£129 000 = 100% of value

10% + 12% = 112%
> We want to find 12% of £129 000 and then add it to £129 000. This is the same as finding 112% of £129 000.

2007 → 2010 = 3 years
> We need to find the increase over three years, so 3 is the power.

$(112\%)^3 \times £129\,000$

$= 1 \cdot 12^3 \times £129\,000$
> Write the calculation as you'll enter it into your calculator.

$= £181\,235 \cdot 71$
> Evaluate the answer.

Example

Bacteria in a Petri dish increase at the rate of 0·8% per hour.
At 1pm, there are 3000 bacteria.
At 5pm, how many bacteria will be present?
Give your answer to three significant figures.

Solution

3000 bacteria = 100%
> Establish the values you'll be using.

100% + 0·8% = 100·8%

1pm → 5pm = 4 hours

$(100\cdot8\%)^4 \times 3000 = 1\cdot008^4 \times 3000$
> Set up the calculation. Be careful that you don't write 1·08 (108%) instead of 1·008 (100·8%).

$= 3097 \ldots$
> Evaluate your answer.

= 3100 bacteria   (3 sig figs)
> Remember to round to 3 sig figs.

Depreciation and Percentage Decrease

When the value of an item decreases over a period of time, it's said to depreciate.

Example

A car which costs £9500 today is thought to depreciate by 20% per annum over the next 4 years. What will it be worth in 4 years' time?

Solution

£9500 = 100%

100% − 20% = 80%
▸ We want to find 20% of £9500 and then subtract it from £9500.
This is the same as finding 80% of £9500.

$(80\%)^4 \times £9500$
▸ We need to find the decrease over 4 years, so the power is 4.

$= (0.8)^4 \times £9500$
▸ Write the calculation as you'll enter it into your calculator.

$= £3891.20$
▸ Evaluate the answer.

Example

A patient is given 200 milligrams of a drug at 9am. The amount of the drug in the blood decreases at a rate of 15% per hour.

How much of the drug will be in the patient's blood by 12 noon?

Solution

9am → 12 noon = 3 hrs
▸ Establish your values and set up your calculation.

$(85\%)^3 \times 200 \text{ mg} = 0.85^3 \times 200 \text{ mg}$
▸ Write the calculation as you'll enter it into your calculator.

$= 122.825 \text{ mg}$
▸ Evaluate the answer.

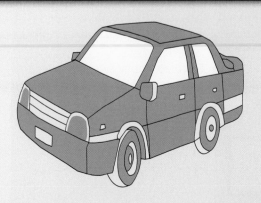

Percentages – Finding the Original Amount

Sometimes we are told the new value of an item and asked to find the original value before the percentage increase has been added on. The easiest way to do this is to make an equation of the information and then substitute in what you know.

For example, cost of meal before VAT × 1·15 = cost of meal including VAT

Example

A jar of chocolate spread is on special offer and contains 12·5% more than a normal jar. The special-offer jar contains 630 g of chocolate spread. How much would a normal jar contain?

Solution

normal jar × 1·125 = special-offer jar ▶ Set up the equation.

normal jar × 1·125 = 630 ▶ Substitute in the values you know.

$$\text{normal jar} = \frac{630}{1\cdot125}$$ ▶ Get the unknown on its own.

= 560 g ▶ Calculate the answer.

This question could also be answered without using a calculator. If you come across this type of question in a non-calculator paper, then you have to convert the percentage into its equivalent fraction.

$$25\% = \frac{1}{4} \to 12\cdot5\% = \frac{1}{8} \to 112\cdot5\% = 1\frac{1}{8}$$

normal jar × $1\frac{1}{8}$ = special-offer jar ▶ Set up the equation.

normal jar × $1\frac{1}{8}$ = 630 ▶ Substitute in the values you know.

normal jar × $\frac{9}{8}$ = 630 ▶ Make the fraction top-heavy.

normal jar = 630 ÷ $\frac{9}{8}$ ▶ Get the unknown on its own.

normal jar = 630 × $\frac{8}{9}$ ▶ Multiply and flip the fraction.

normal jar = 70 × $\frac{8}{1}$ ▶ Simplify if possible before multiplying.

= 560 g ▶ Calculate the answer.

Look out for

Always think to yourself: 'Is my answer sensible?'

Ratio

Ratios can be used to compare, mix or share quantities. Each part of the ratio should be in the same units and in its simplest form.

Example

Lesley bakes shortbread to sell to her local coffee shop. Her recipe uses flour, sugar and butter in a ratio of 3:1:2.

(a) How much of each ingredient is needed to make 9 kg of shortbread?

Solution

3:1:2 → 6 parts	▶ Add all the parts of the ratio together.
9 kg ÷ 6 = 1·5 kg	▶ Divide down to find out the value of one part.
Flour = 3 × 1·5 = 4·5 kg	▶ Multiply each ingredient by its given ratio.
Sugar = 1 × 1·5 kg = 1·5 kg	
Butter = 2 × 1·5 = 3 kg	
(Check: 4·5 + 1·5 + 3 = 9 kg)	▶ You don't need to show the checking line, but it's worth doing to see if you've made a mistake anywhere.

Example

(b) She buys flour for £1·14 per kilogram, sugar for £0·92 per kilogram and butter for £3·82 per kilogram. If Lesley sells the shortbread for £3·75 per kilogram, how much profit does she make?

Solution

Flour = £1·14 × 4·5 kg = £5·13 Sugar = £0·92 × 1·5 kg = £1·38 Butter = £3·82 × 3 kg = £11·46	▶ Multiply the quantity of each ingredient by the price per kilogram.
Total cost = £5·13 + £1·38 + £11·46 = £17·97	▶ Add the three prices together to get a total cost of making the shortbread.
Selling price = £3·75 × 9 kg = £33·75	▶ Calculate the selling price.
Profit = £33·75 − £17·97 = £15·78	▶ Subtract the selling price from the total cost to calculate the profit.

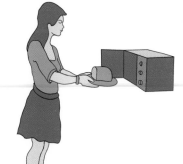

Variation (Proportion)

As soon as you read 'y varies directly as x' or 'y is proportional to x' in a question, you can instantly write down:

$$y \propto x$$
$$\text{so } y = kx \qquad (k \text{ is a constant})$$

Most often, this type of question will require you firstly to find the value of k, then to use it to state a formula connecting x and y.

There are three types of variation (proportion): Direct, Inverse and Joint.

Look out for

These types of questions often have a lot of text and information – but don't let that put you off. Look out for the key words and figures; it may help you to highlight them. The order that the information appears in is the order in which you'll put it into the formula.

Direct Variation

Direct variation means that, as one quantity increases, the other quantity increases OR as one quantity decreases, the other quantity decreases too.

For example, as the number of packets of crisps increases, the total cost increases.
So, if one packet of crisps costs 30 pence, then five packets will cost £1·50.

Example
The distance travelled (d metres) by a snowboarder varies directly to the square of the time (t seconds). A snowboarder can cover 24 metres in 2 seconds.

(a) Find a formula for d in terms of t.

Solution

$d = 24 \quad t = 2$ ▸ State the values of d and t. This helps you to make the correct substitution.

$d \propto t^2$ ▸ Write your statement in mathematical terms.

$d = kt^2$ ▸ Replace $\propto$ with '$= k$'.

$24 = k \times 2^2$ ▸ Substitute in the values of d and t stated above.

$24 = k \times 4$

$k = \dfrac{24}{4}$ ▸ Rearrange to find the value of k.

$k = 6$

$\Rightarrow d = 6t^2$ ▸ State the formula.

continued

Direct Variation – continued

Example

(b) How long does it take the snowboarder to travel 1350 metres?

Solution

$$d = 1350 \text{ m}$$ ▸ State the values you know.

$$d = 6t^2$$ ▸ State the formula.

$$1350 = 6t^2$$ ▸ Substitute into the formula.

$$\frac{1350}{6} = t^2$$ ▸ Solve to find the unknown. Remember to check that your units are sensible.

$$t^2 = 225$$

$$t = \sqrt{225}$$

$$\text{time} = 15 \text{ secs}$$

Inverse Variation

Inverse variation means that, as one quantity increases, the other quantity decreases OR as one quantity decreases, the other quantity increases.

For example, as the number of people digging a garden increases, the time taken decreases.

So, if one person takes eight hours to dig, then four people will take two hours.

Example

When a tyre is punctured, the air pressure (P units) varies inversely as the square root of the time, t, in seconds. Neil drives over a nail. Four seconds after the puncture, the tyre pressure is 26 units. What is the tyre pressure 20 seconds after the puncture?

Solution

$$P = 26 \quad t = 4$$ ▸ State the values of P and t.

$$P \propto \frac{1}{\sqrt{t}}$$ ▸ Write your statement in mathematical terms.

$$P = \frac{k}{\sqrt{t}}$$ ▸ Replace $\propto$ with '$= k$'.

$$26 = \frac{k}{\sqrt{4}}$$ ▸ Substitute in the values of P and t stated above.

$$26 = \frac{k}{2}$$ ▸ Rearrange to find the value of k.

$$k = 52$$

$$\Rightarrow P = \frac{52}{\sqrt{t}}$$ ▸ State the formula.

$$t = 20$$ ▸ State the value of t.

$$P = \frac{52}{\sqrt{20}}$$ ▸ Substitute in t.

$$P = 11 \cdot 627 \ldots$$ ▸ Solve to find P.

Air pressure = 11·6 units

Joint Variation

Joint variation can be made up of:
- more than one type of direct proportion
- more than one type of inverse proportion
- a mixture of direct and inverse proportion.

Example

The time, t (minutes), taken for a rugby stadium to empty varies directly as the number of fans, F, and inversely as the number of gates, G, which are open.

It takes 15 minutes for a stadium to empty when there are 30 000 fans and 25 gates open.

(a) Find a formula connecting t, F and G.

Solution

$t = 15 \quad F = 30\,000 \quad G = 25$	State the values of t, F and G.
$t \, \alpha \, \dfrac{F}{G}$	Write your statement in mathematical terms.
$t = \dfrac{kF}{G}$	Replace α with '$= k$'.
$15 = \dfrac{k \times 30\,000}{25}$	Substitute in the values of t, F and G stated above.
$375 = k \times 30\,000$	
$k = \dfrac{375}{30\,000}$	Rearrange to find the value of k. It's often easier to use the number as a fraction.
$= \dfrac{1}{80}$ (or 0·0125)	
$\Rightarrow t = \dfrac{F}{80G}$	State the formula.

Example

(b) How many fans are at the game if it takes 10 minutes to empty the stadium with 20 gates open?

Solution

$t = 10 \quad G = 20$	State the values of t and G.
$t = \dfrac{F}{80G}$	State the formula.
$10 = \dfrac{F}{80 \times 20}$	Substitute in t and G.
$10 = \dfrac{F}{1600}$	Rearrange to find the value of F.
$F = 16000$ fans	

Patterns

Example

Consecutive cubic numbers can be added using the following pattern.

$$1^3 + 2^3 = \frac{2^2 \times 3^2}{4}$$

$$1^3 + 2^3 + 3^3 = \frac{3^2 \times 4^2}{4}$$

$$1^3 + 2^3 + 3^3 + 4^3 = \frac{4^2 \times 5^2}{4}$$

(a) Express $1^3 + 2^3 + 3^3 + 4^3 + 5^3 + 6^3 + 7^3$ in the same way.

Solution

$$1^3 + 2^3 + 3^3 + 4^3 = \frac{4^2 \times 5^2}{4}$$

$$1^3 + 2^3 + 3^3 + 4^3 + 5^3 = \frac{5^2 \times 6^2}{4}$$

$$1^3 + 2^3 + 3^3 + 4^3 + 5^3 + 6^3 = \frac{6^2 \times 7^2}{4}$$

$$1^3 + 2^3 + 3^3 + 4^3 + 5^3 + 6^3 + 7^3 = \frac{7^2 \times 8^2}{4}$$

▶ You may find it helpful to continue the pattern to answer this part of the question. If you understand the pattern and can go straight to stating the answer, then it's unnecessary to show the three lines in green.

Example

(b) Write down an expression for the sum of the first n consecutive cubic numbers.

Solution

$$\frac{n^2(n + 1)^2}{4}$$

▶ n is the number of terms being added together.

For example:

$$\underbrace{1^3 + 2^3 + 3^3}_{3 \text{ terms}} = \frac{3^2 \times 4^2}{4}$$

So, if $n = 3$:

$n^2 \qquad (n^2 + 1)^2$ Since $3 + 1 = 4$

$$\underbrace{1^3 + 2^3 + 3^3}_{n \text{ terms}} = \frac{3^2 \times 4^2}{4}$$

continued

continued

Example

(c) Write down an expression for $8^3 + 9^3 + 10^3 + \ldots n^3$.

Solution

$$1^3 + 2^3 + \ldots + n^3 = \frac{n^2(n+1)^2}{4}$$

▶ The last term in the pattern is n^3, and the sum of the first n terms is the answer from part (b).

$$1^3 + 2^3 + \ldots + 7^3 = \frac{7^2 \times 8^2}{4}$$

▶ This pattern starts at 8^3 which means $1^3 + 2^3 + \ldots + 7^3$ are not included. We know the expression for the sum of the first seven terms from part (a).

$$\Rightarrow 8^3 + 9^3 + 10^3 + \ldots + n^3 = \frac{n^2(n+1)^2 - 7^2 \times 8^2}{4}$$

▶ The final answer is the answer to part (b) subtracting part (a).

Look out for

You should always be able to answer part (a) by continuing the pattern. All the clues to answer the question are on the page.

Example

A sequence of terms, starting with 1, is

1, 5, 9, 13, 17, … .

Consecutive terms in this sequence are formed by adding 4 to the previous term.

The total of consecutive terms of this sequence can be found using the following pattern.

Total of the first 2 terms:	1 + 5	= 2 × 3
Total of the first 3 terms:	1 + 5 + 9	= 3 × 5
Total of the first 4 terms:	1 + 5 + 9 + 13	= 4 × 7
Total of the first 5 terms:	1 + 5 + 9 + 13 + 17	= 5 × 9

(a) Express the total of the first nine terms of this sequence in the same way.

Solution

Total of the first 6 terms:	1 + 5 + 9 + 13 + 17 + 21	= 6 × 11
Total of the first 7 terms:	1 + 5 + 9 + 13 + 17 + 21 + 25	= 7 × 13
Total of the first 8 terms:	1 + 5 + 9 + 13 + 17 + 21 + 25 + 29	= 8 × 15
Total of the first 9 terms:	1 + 5 + 9 + 13 + 17 + 21 + 25 + 29 + 33	= 9 × 17

continued

continued

> Continue the pattern until you reach the ninth term.

> If you are able to go straight to the answer, then it isn't necessary to include the lines in green.

Example

(b) The first n terms of this sequence are added together. Write down an expression, in n, for the total.

Solution

Total of the first 10 terms: $1 + 5 + ...$ $= 10 \times 19$

Total of the first 11 terms: $1 + 5 + ...$ $= 11 \times 21$

Total of the first 12 terms: $1 + 5 + ...$ $= 12 \times 23$

Total of the first n terms: $1 + 5 + ...$ $= n(2n - 1)$

> Continue the pattern until you can spot what the rule is. If you are able to go straight to the answer, then do so.

Substitution

Substitution in maths is really just the same as when you use a substitute in sport, but, instead of replacing one player by another, you replace a letter by a number.

Example

$B = 3a^2 - c^2$

Calculate B when $a = 2$ and $c = -5$

Solution

$B = 3 \times 2^2 - (-5)^2$ ▶ Substitute in values.

$\quad = 3 \times 4 - 25$ ▶ Evaluate each part – take care with the negatives.

$\quad = 12 - 25$ ▶ Work out your answer.

$\quad = -13$

Example

(a) $f(x) = 10 - 3x$

Evaluate $f(-4)$.

Solution

$f(-4) = 10 - (3 \times -4)$ ▶ Substitute in values.

$\quad = 10 - (-12)$ ▶ Evaluate each part – take care with the negatives.

$\quad = 10 + 12$ ▶ Work out your answer.

$\quad = 22$

(b) Given that $f(a) = 11$, find a.

Solution

$f(a) = 10 - 3a$ ▶ Substitute a into $f(x)$.

$10 - 3a = 11$ ▶ Set the two expressions for $f(a)$ equal to each other.

$-3a = 1$ ▶ Solve the equation to find a.

$a = -\dfrac{1}{3}$

Formulae

When evaluating a formula, it is essential that you remember the order of operations (see BODMAS: page 6).

Example

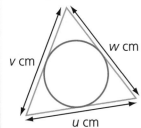

A circle can be drawn inside a triangle, as shown in the diagram.

The radius, r centimetres, of this circle can be found using the formula

$$r = \sqrt{\frac{(s-u)(s-v)(s-w)}{s}}, \text{ where } s = \frac{1}{2}(u+v+w).$$

Use this formula to find the radius of the circle shown in this diagram:

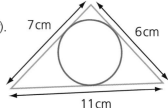

continued

Formula – continued

Solution

$u = 11 \quad v = 7 \quad w = 6$ ▶ State the values of u, v and w.

$s = \frac{1}{2}(u + v + w)$ ▶ State the formula for s.

$= \frac{1}{2}(11 + 7 + 6)$ ▶ Substitute into the formula for s.

$= \frac{1}{2}(24)$ ▶ Calculate s.

$= 12$

$r = \sqrt{\dfrac{(s-u)(s-v)(s-w)}{s}}$ ▶ State the formula for r.

$= \sqrt{\dfrac{(12-11)(12-7)(12-6)}{12}}$ ▶ Substitute in the values.

$= \sqrt{\left(\dfrac{30}{12}\right)}$ ▶ Evaluate the numerator and denominator. Put a bracket around $\frac{30}{12}$ so that you square-root the whole fraction and not just 30.

radius = 1·58 cm   ▶ Calculate r.

Look out for

Don't include units in a formula.

Example

Lynsay has a mobile phone. She pays a fixed price of £10 per month for 200 text messages. If she exceeds 200 texts in a month, she is then charged 12 pence per text.

(a) How much does Lynsay pay for texts in a month when she sends 235 texts?

Solution

Total cost = $10 + 0·12(235 - 200)$ ▶ £10 is charged every month.
▶ 200 minutes are free, so we subtract them from the total number of texts sent.

$= 10 + 4·2$ ▶ Multiply the number of texts being charged for by £0·12.

$= £14·20$ ▶ Calculate the answer – remember to include the units.

Example

(b) Write down a formula for the total cost, £C, Lynsay is charged for texts in a month when the number of texts, t, she sends is greater than 200.

Solution

$C = 10 + 0·12(t - 200)$ ▶ We want a formula for the total cost so that we know what C equals.
▶ £10 is a standard charge each month.
▶ £0·12 is charged on each text that Lynsay pays for.
▶ $(t - 200)$ works out how many texts Lynsay pays for.

$C = 10 + 0·12t - 24$ ▶ Multiply out the brackets and simplify.
$C = 0·12t - 14$

(Check: $C = 0·12 \times 235 - 14 = £14·20$ ▶ Check that the formula works for 235 texts.
which is the same as above)

Multiplying Expressions

When you are asked to simplify an expression, be careful with any negatives. Remember that the negative on the outside of a bracket multiplies **everything** inside it.

Look out for

$-(x + 2)$ means that you multiply everything inside the bracket by -1.

Example

Simplify $2(3 - 4x) - 3(5 - 4x)$

Solution

$2(3 - 4x) - 3(5 - 4x)$

$= 6 - 8x - 15 + 12x$ ▶ Multiply out each bracket. Notice that the second bracket is multiplied by -3.

$= 4x - 9$ ▶ Collect like terms.

Example

Expand and simplify $(x - 1)(x^2 + 3x - 10)$

Solution

$(x - 1)(x^2 + 3x - 10)$

$= x^3 + 3x^2 - 10x - x^2 - 3x + 10$ ▶ Multiply everything in the second bracket by x: $x(x^2 + 3x - 10) = x^3 + 3x^2 - 10x$

▶ Multiply everything in the second bracket by -1: $-1(x^2 + 3x - 10) = -x^2 - 3x + 10$

$= x^3 + 2x^2 - 13x + 10$ ▶ Collect like terms.

The brackets can also be expanded using a table if you find it easier:

	x^2	$+3x$	-10
x	x^3	$+3x^2$	$-10x$
-1	$-x^2$	$-3x$	$+10$

Algebraic Fractions

Basic rules

The rules for working with algebraic fractions are exactly the same as those for numerical fractions.

We must always have a common denominator to add or subtract fractions. The easiest way to do this is to multiply fraction 1 by the denominator of fraction 2 and vice versa.

Look out for

Always give your answer over one denominator and make sure that the line underlines everything that is on both the top and the bottom of the fraction.

For example: $\dfrac{3}{2x} + \dfrac{x}{4}$

$$= \dfrac{4 \times 3}{4 \times 2x} + \dfrac{2x \times x}{2x \times 4}$$

$$= \dfrac{12}{8x} + \dfrac{2x^2}{8x}$$

$$= \dfrac{12 + 2x^2}{8x}$$

Look out for

Just like numerical fractions, algebraic fractions should always be given in their simplest form. Factorising the numerator and denominator, when possible, will allow you to see if you can simplify.

For example: $\dfrac{12 + 2x^2}{8x}$

$$= \dfrac{2(6 + x^2)}{8x}$$

$$= \dfrac{6 + x^2}{4x}$$

Example

Simplify $\dfrac{4}{x-1} - \dfrac{2}{x}$

Solution

$$\dfrac{4x}{x(x-1)} - \dfrac{2(x-1)}{x(x-1)}$$
▶ Get a common denominator by multiplying top and bottom by the other denominator.

$$= \dfrac{4x - 2(x-1)}{x(x-1)}$$
▶ Put over one denominator.

$$= \dfrac{4x - 2x + 2}{x(x-1)}$$
▶ Expand the bracket on the top line. Be careful of the negative!

$$= \dfrac{2x + 2}{x(x-1)}$$
▶ Simplify the numerator.

$$= \dfrac{2(x+1)}{x(x-1)}$$
▶ Factorise the top line, and, if possible, simplify.

21

Factorising

When you are asked to factorise, you must always follow these three steps in order: common factor, difference of two squares and quadratic.

- a common factor, eg: $2x - 6 = 2(x - 3)$
- a difference of two squares, eg: $x^2 - 25 = (x + 5)(x - 5)$
- a quadratic (trinomial), eg: $x^2 + x - 6 = (x + 3)(x - 2)$

Look out for

Remember the order of the brackets doesn't matter.

Example

(a) Factorise $9x^2 - y^2$

Solution $9x^2 - y^2$ ▸ Look for a common factor – there isn't one.

$(3x)^2 - y^2$ ▸ Look for a difference of two squares (two square terms being subtracted) – this is the case!

$= (3x + y)(3x - y)$ ▸ Square-root each term and put into two sets of brackets – one adding, the other subtracting.

Look out for

'Hence' means that you're going to have to use your answer from an earlier part of the question.

(b) Hence simplify: $\dfrac{9x^2 - y^2}{6x + 2y}$

Solution

$\dfrac{(3x + y)(3x - y)}{2(3x + y)}$ ▸ Replace the numerator with the answer from part (a).
▸ Factorise the denominator – a common factor.

$= \dfrac{3x - y}{2}$ ▸ Cancel the matching brackets on the top and bottom to leave the simplified answer.

Look out for

A factor on the top line should always be identical to a factor on the bottom line to allow simplification to occur.

Example

Factorise $2x^2 - 5x - 3$

Solution

$2x^2 - 5x - 3$ ▸ Think of the factors of $2x^2$: $2x$ and x
$= (2x + 1)(x - 3)$ ▸ Think of the factors of -3: 1 and -3, -1 and 3
▸ You should be able to spot what goes where – but, if not, you can use trial and error to get your answer.
▸ Always multiply out your brackets to make sure you obtain what you started with. If you don't arrive back at the original expression, then you've made a mistake.

Check: $2x^2 - 6x + x - 3 = 2x^2 - 5x - 3$

Equations

Linear Equations

A linear equation is an equation where the highest power of x is 1.

For example: $x + 1 = 5$, $2x - 3 = -11$, $-3x + 12 = 7$.

When solving linear equations, you should only ever have one answer.

Example

Solve $2x - 3(x + 1) = 5$

Solution

$$2x - 3(x + 1) = 5$$

$$2x - 3x - 3 = 5$$
▶ Expand the bracket, taking care with the negative.

$$-x - 3 = 5$$
▶ Collect like terms.

$$-x = 8$$
▶ Add 3 to both sides.

$$x = -8$$
▶ Divide both sides by -1.

Example

Solve $\dfrac{3}{x} - 2 = 5$

Solution

$$\dfrac{3}{x} - 2 = 5$$

$$\dfrac{3}{x} = 7$$
▶ Add 2 to both sides.

$$3 = 7x$$
▶ Multiply both sides by x.

$$x = \dfrac{3}{7}$$
▶ Divide both sides by 7.

Example

Solve $\dfrac{x}{3} - \dfrac{(x+2)}{4} = 1$

Solution

$$\dfrac{x}{3} - \dfrac{(x+2)}{4} = 1$$

$$x - 3\dfrac{(x+2)}{4} = 3$$
▶ Multiply all the terms by 3.

$$4x - 3(x + 2) = 12$$
▶ Multiply all the terms by 4.

$$4x - 3x - 6 = 12$$
▶ Expand the bracket.

$$x - 6 = 12$$
▶ Collect like terms.

$$x = 18$$
▶ Add 6 to both sides.

continued

Linear Equations – continued

Solution

You could also answer the previous question by finding a common denominator.

$$\frac{x}{3} - \frac{x+2}{4} = 1$$

$$\frac{4x}{12} - 3\frac{(x+2)}{12} = 1$$ ▶ Multiply $\frac{x}{3}$ by $\frac{4}{4}$ and $\frac{x+2}{4}$ by $\frac{3}{3}$ to give a common denominator of 12.

$$\frac{4x - 3(x+2)}{12} = 1$$ ▶ Put over one denominator.

$$\frac{4x - 3x - 6}{12} = 1$$ ▶ Expand the bracket on the top line.

$$\frac{x - 6}{12} = 1$$ ▶ Simplify the top line.

$$x - 6 = 12$$ ▶ Multiply both sides by 12.

$$x = 18$$ ▶ Solve to find x.

Quadratic Equations

A quadratic equation is an equation where the highest power of x is 2.
For example: $x^2 = 5$, $\quad x^2 + 1 = 12$, $\quad -3x^2 + 10 = -2$, $\quad (2x + 1)^2 = 9$.
When solving quadratic equations, you should have, at the most, two answers.
To solve a quadratic equation, always have the equation in the general form $ax^2 + bx + c = 0$ before you begin to solve.

Example

Solve $y^2 = 5y$

Solution

$$y^2 = 5y$$

$$y^2 - 5y = 0$$ ▶ Bring all the terms to one side and have the equation equal to zero (that is, in the form $ax^2 + bx + c = 0$).

$$y(y - 5) = 0$$ ▶ Take out a common factor. Check to see if it can be factorised further. In this case, it can't.

$$y = 0 \text{ or } y - 5 = 0$$ ▶ Set each part equal to zero, and solve.

$$y = 5$$

continued

Look out for

$y^2 = 5y$ is a quadratic equation. A common mistake in this question is to cancel the y's on either side of the equals sign, leaving $y = 5$ as the only answer. To solve any quadratic equation, you must set it equal to zero, and solve to find the two solutions.

Quadratic Equations – continued

Example

Solve $x^2 + 2x - 6 = 6x - 1$

Solution

$$x^2 + 2x - 6 = 6x - 1$$

$x^2 + 2x - 6 - 6x + 1 = 0$ ▸ Collect all the terms on one side and have the equation equal to zero (that is, in the form $ax^2 + bx + c = 0$).

$x^2 - 4x - 5 = 0$ ▸ Collect like terms.

$(x - 5)(x + 1) = 0$ ▸ Factorise.

$x - 5 = 0$ or $x + 1 = 0$ ▸ Set each bracket equal to zero, and solve.

$x = 5$ $x = -1$

Inequalities

Inequalities should be treated in the same way as equations. The only exception to this is multiplying or dividing by a negative number. To avoid confusion about this matter, it is easiest to add (or subtract) the smaller number of x's.

Example

Solve the following inequality: $1 + 3x \geq 5x + 5$

Solution

$1 + 3x \geq 5x + 5$

$1 \geq 2x + 5$ ▸ $3x$ is smaller than $5x$, so subtract $3x$ from both sides.

$-4 \geq 2x$ ▸ Subtract 5 from both sides.

$-2 \geq x$ ▸ Divide both sides by 2.

$x \leq -2$

Example

Solve $2 - x < 3(x + 4)$

Solution

$2 - x < 3x + 12$ ▸ Expand the bracket.

$2 < 4x + 12$ ▸ $-x$ is smaller than $3x$, so add x to each side.

$-10 < 4x$ ▸ Subtract 12 from both sides.

$\dfrac{-10}{4} < x$ ▸ Divide both sides by 4.

$-\dfrac{5}{2} < x$ ▸ Simplify. Leave your answer as a fraction.

$x > -\dfrac{5}{2}$

Quadratic Formula

Not every quadratic equation can be factorised using the three methods. An alternative method for factorising a quadratic equation is the Quadratic Formula. A hint to use it can be the question asking you to round to one or two decimal places or to a number of significant figures (see page 22).

The quadratic formula is $x = \dfrac{-b \pm \sqrt{b^2 - 4ac}}{2a}$ (It's given on the formula sheet!)

The quadratic equation needs to be in the form $ax^2 + bx + c = 0$ ($a \neq 0$). It tends to be given in this format, but there's no guarantee, so be careful!

If $b^2 - 4ac$ works out to be negative, then it means that x has no real solutions. Go back and check that the values of a, b and c are correct (including the sign) and that $b^2 - 4ac$ has been correctly calculated.

Example

Solve the equation $x^2 + 5x - 4 = 0$

Give your answer to one decimal place.

Solution

$x^2 + 5x - 4 = 0$

▸ Compare equation with $ax^2 + bx + c$.

$a = 1 \quad b = 5 \quad c = -4$

▸ State the values of a, b and c.

$x = \dfrac{-b \pm \sqrt{b^2 - 4ac}}{2a}$

▸ Substitute into the formula. (Remember it's on the formula sheet.)

$= \dfrac{-5 \pm \sqrt{5^2 - 4 \times 1 \times -4}}{2 \times 1}$

$\begin{aligned} b^2 - 4ac &= 5^2 - 4 \times 1 \times -4 \\ &= 41 \end{aligned}$

▸ At the side, work out $b^2 - 4ac$.

$= \dfrac{-5 \pm \sqrt{41}}{2}$

▸ Leave your answer as a surd and substitute back into the formula.

$x = \dfrac{-5 - \sqrt{41}}{2}$ or $x = \dfrac{-5 + \sqrt{41}}{2}$

$= -5 \cdot 701 \ldots$ $\qquad = 0 \cdot 701 \ldots$

$= -5 \cdot 7$ $\qquad\qquad = 0 \cdot 7$

▸ Separate your two solutions and work each out. Be careful to use brackets around the top line when you enter it into your calculator. Alternatively work out the top line before dividing by 2.

▸ Remember to round accordingly.

Simultaneous Equations

A simultaneous equation is when you have two equations, each with two unknowns. There are different ways you can solve these, but the process of elimination tends to be the most common.

You are most likely to meet simultaneous equations in the context of a problem, and you should follow these steps to answer the question:

1. State clearly the two equations you are going to use.
2. You are less likely to make a mistake if you always add your two equations. This means that one of the terms will be positive and its like term in the other equation will be negative.
3. Solve to find one of your unknown values.
4. Substitute this value into either of the original equations to find the other unknown.
5. State your answer.

Example

Bell High School is selling tickets for the end-of-term talent show. The Struthers family buys two adult and three child tickets costing a total of £10·25. The Maciver family buys three adult and four child tickets costing a total of £14·50. What price is each ticket?

Solution

Let a = cost of an adult ticket
$\quad c$ = cost of a child ticket

$2a + 3c = 10{\cdot}25 \qquad ① \times 3$
$3a + 4c = 14{\cdot}50 \qquad ② \times -2$
▶ Set up your two equations and label them.

$6a + 9c = 30{\cdot}75 \qquad ③$
$-6a - 8c = -29 \qquad ④$
▶ By multiplying the equations to give you a positive and a negative like term, you can eliminate a.

$$
\begin{array}{rrrrr}
6a & + & 9c & = & 30{\cdot}75 \\
-6a & - & 8c & = & -29 \\
\hline
0 & + & c & = & 1{\cdot}75
\end{array}
$$
▶ Add the two new equations.

$③ + ④: \ c = 1{\cdot}75$

Substitute into ①: $2a + 3 \times 1{\cdot}75 = 10{\cdot}25$
$\qquad\qquad\qquad 2a + 5{\cdot}25 = 10{\cdot}25$
$\qquad\qquad\qquad\qquad 2a = 5$
$\qquad\qquad\qquad\qquad\quad = 2{\cdot}5$
▶ Substitute the value of c into either of the original equations.
▶ Solve to find the value of a.

An adult ticket costs £2·50 and a child's ticket costs £1·75.
▶ State your answer in a sentence.

Look out for

Always write a sentence stating your answer to finish the question.

Changing the Subject

When changing the subject of a formula, you use the same strategies involved in solving equations.

For example, $V = \pi r^2 h$ is the formula for finding the volume of a cylinder when the radius (r) and the height (h) are known. V, the volume, is called the subject of the formula. If we know the volume and height of the cylinder and want to find the radius, then we can rearrange the formula to make r the subject.

Example

Change the subject of the formula below to q.

$$p = \frac{q^2 + r}{3}$$

Solution

$p = \dfrac{q^2 + r}{3}$

$3p = q^2 + r$ ▶ Multiply both sides by 3.

$3p - r = q^2$ ▶ Subtract r from both sides.

$q = \sqrt{3p - r}$ ▶ Square-root both sides.

Look out for

Make sure the square root sign covers everything being square-rooted!

Surds

Reminder: Square numbers: 1, 4, 16, 25, 36, 49, 64, …

When we cannot work out the root of a number exactly, we call it a surd. We treat surds using the same principles of algebra (that is, you can only add like to like or subtract like from like). We can simplify a surd using the square number which is a factor of the original value.

For example, $\sqrt{12} = \sqrt{4 \times 3} = \sqrt{4}\sqrt{3} = 2\sqrt{3}$

$2\sqrt{18} = 2\sqrt{9 \times 2} = 2\sqrt{9}\sqrt{2} = 2 \times 3\sqrt{2} = 6\sqrt{2}$

Example

Simplify $\sqrt{18} + 2\sqrt{2}$

Solution

$\sqrt{9 \times 2} + 2\sqrt{2}$ ▶ Find a square number that is a factor of 18.

$= \sqrt{9}\sqrt{2} + 2\sqrt{2}$ 9×2 is 18, so $\sqrt{18}$ is the same as $\sqrt{9}\sqrt{2}$.

$= 3\sqrt{2} + 2\sqrt{2}$ ▶ Evaluate $\sqrt{9}$.

$= 5\sqrt{2}$ ▶ Simplify to give the answer.

continued

continued

Example

Evaluate $\dfrac{\sqrt{24}}{\sqrt{3}}$

Usually, there's a hint in the question as to what number will be under the square-root sign in the answer.

Solution

$$\dfrac{\sqrt{24}}{\sqrt{3}}$$

$$= \dfrac{\sqrt{8}\sqrt{3}}{\sqrt{3}}$$ ▶ Use the hint from the question to find the factors of 24.

$$= \sqrt{8}$$ ▶ Cancel $\sqrt{3}$ on top and bottom.

$$= \sqrt{4}\sqrt{2}$$ ▶ Find a square number which is a factor of 8.

$$= 2\sqrt{2}$$ ▶ Simplify $\sqrt{4}$.

When you are asked to **rationalise a denominator**, you are being asked to get rid of the surd on the bottom line. To do this, you must multiply top and bottom by the surd.

Remember that $\sqrt{x} \times \sqrt{x} = \sqrt{x \times x} = \sqrt{x^2} = x$

Example

Simplify $\dfrac{\sqrt{2}}{\sqrt{24}}$

Express your answer as a fraction with a rational denominator.

Solution

$$\dfrac{\sqrt{2}}{\sqrt{24}}$$

$$= \dfrac{\sqrt{2}}{\sqrt{2}\sqrt{12}}$$ ▶ Split $\sqrt{24}$ into parts involving $\sqrt{2}$.

$$= \dfrac{1}{\sqrt{12}}$$ ▶ Cancel $\sqrt{2}$ top and bottom.

$$= \dfrac{\sqrt{12}}{12}$$ ▶ Multiply top and bottom by $\sqrt{12}$.

$$= \dfrac{\sqrt{4}\sqrt{3}}{12}$$ ▶ Simplify $\sqrt{12}$.

$$= \dfrac{2\sqrt{3}}{12}$$ ▶ Simplify fully.

$$= \dfrac{\sqrt{3}}{6}$$

Using the difference of two squares, we know that

$$(x + \sqrt{y})(x - \sqrt{y}) = x^2 - (\sqrt{y})^2 = x^2 - y$$

$(x + \sqrt{y})$ and $(x - \sqrt{y})$ are **conjugates** of each other. When we multiply them together, their product is rational (that means it doesn't contain any surds).

When we are asked to rationalise a denominator of the form $(x \pm \sqrt{y})$, then we multiply the denominator by its conjugate.

Example

Express $\dfrac{2}{3 - \sqrt{5}}$ with a rational denominator.

Solution

$$\frac{2}{3 - \sqrt{5}}$$

$$= \frac{2(3 + \sqrt{5})}{(3 - \sqrt{5})(3 + \sqrt{5})}$$ ▶ Multiply by $(3 + \sqrt{5})$ which is the conjugate of $(3 - \sqrt{5})$.

$$= \frac{2(3 + \sqrt{5})}{9 - 5}$$ ▶ Use the difference of two squares to multiply out the brackets on the denominator.

$$= \frac{2(3 + \sqrt{5})}{4}$$ ▶ Simplify.

$$= \frac{3 + \sqrt{5}}{2}$$

Look out for !

Always fully simplify an answer – even if the question doesn't ask you to.

Indices

Indices are powers. On x^n, x is the base and n is the power, or index.

You must know the following rules.

1. To multiply terms with the same base, add the powers: $\quad\quad\quad x^a \times x^b = x^{a+b}$

2. To divide terms with the same base, subtract the powers:
$$\frac{x^a}{x^b} = x^{a-b}$$
$$x^a \div x^b = x^{a-b}$$

3. To find the power of a power, multiply the powers: $\quad\quad (x^a)^b = x^{ab}$

4. Any base to the power zero is 1: $\quad\quad\quad\quad\quad\quad\quad x^0 = 1$

5. $x^{-1} = \dfrac{1}{x}$

$\quad x^{-a} = \dfrac{1}{x^a}$

6. $x^{\frac{1}{a}} = \sqrt[a]{x}$

$\quad x^{\frac{a}{b}} = \sqrt{x} = x^{1/2} = \sqrt[b]{x^a}$

▶ This rule can be remembered by using the memory aid OBIT.

> Outside
> Bottom
> Inside
> Top
>
> Inside goes to Top of fraction
>
> $\left(\sqrt[4]{x^3} = x^{3/4}\right.$
>
> Outside goes to Bottom of fraction

Example

Simplify $\quad a^5 \times (a^{-2})^3$

Solution

$a^5 \times (a^{-2})^3$

$= a^5 \times a^{-6}$ $\quad$ ▶ Multiply –2 and 3.

$= a^{-1}$ $\quad\quad\quad$ ▶ Add 5 and –6.

$\left(= \dfrac{1}{a}\right)$ $\quad\quad$ ▶ The line in green is not necessary unless the question asked you to give your answer with a positive index.

Example

Evaluate $\quad 27^{\frac{2}{3}}$

Solution

$27^{\frac{2}{3}}$

$= \sqrt[3]{27}^2$ $\quad$ ▶ Rewrite in surds and indices. Think to yourself: do I know 27^2 or $\sqrt[3]{27}$.

$= 3^2$ $\quad\quad$ ▶ Evaluate $\sqrt[3]{27}$.

$= 9$ $\quad\quad$ ▶ Simplify.

Perimeter

> At Credit level, perimeter questions usually require you to use Pythagoras' Theorem or Trigonometry. Finding the perimeter tends to be the final line of working.

Example

The diagram below shows a table whose top is in the shape of part of a circle with centre O and radius 55 centimetres.

EF is a straight line.

Angle EOF is 90°.

Calculate the perimeter of the table top.

Solution

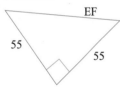

▶ Extract and sketch the right-angled triangle from the diagram, and label the sides.

By Pythagoras: $c^2 = a^2 + b^2$

▶ State Pythagoras' Theorem and substitute into it.

$(EF)^2 = 55^2 + 55^2$

$= 6050$

▶ Find the length of side EF.

$EF = \sqrt{6050}$

$= 77.781 \ldots$

$= 77.78$ cm

Length of arc $= \dfrac{270}{360}\pi d$

▶ 90° of the arc of the circle is missing, so we want to find the length of the arc of 270°.

$= \dfrac{270}{360}\pi \times 110$

▶ Find the length of the arc of the circle.

$= 259.181 \ldots$ cm

$P = 259.181 \ldots + 77.78$

▶ Add the length of the arc to length EF.

$= 336.961 \ldots$

$= 337.0$ cm

The perimeter is 337·0 cm

▶ State the answer.

Area

Area questions at Credit level normally fall into one of two categories:

1. algebra
2. as the lead-in to a volume question. We'll cover this second type when we look at volume.

You have to know the following formulae:

Square $A = l^2$

Rectangle $A = lb$

Triangle $A = \frac{1}{2}bh$

Circle $A = \pi r^2$

Look out for

Straight-edged shapes can be split up into rectangles and triangles.

Look out for

To find the area of any regular polygon, split it into identical triangles, find the area of one triangle and then multiply by the total number of triangles you have.

Example

The area of the triangle below is 6 square centimetres.

It has a base of $(2x + 1)$ centimetres and a height of $2x$ centimetres.

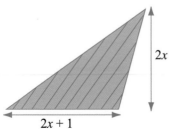

Calculate the value of x.

continued

continued

Solution

$\text{Area } \Delta = \dfrac{1}{2}\text{base} \times \text{height}$ ▶ State the formula for the area of a triangle.

$6 = \dfrac{1}{2}(2x + 1) \times 2x$ ▶ Substitute in the information you know.

$6 = x(2x + 1)$ ▶ Simplify the brackets.

$6 = 2x^2 + x$

$0 = 2x^2 + x - 6$
$2x^2 + x - 6 = 0$
▶ Collect all the terms on one side. It doesn't matter if you leave the terms on the right-hand side and solve from there.

$(2x - 3)(x + 2) = 0$ ▶ Factorise – remember the three methods.

$2x - 3 = 0 \quad \text{or} \quad x + 2 = 0$ ▶ Set each bracket equal to zero, and solve to find two answers.

$\quad 2x = 3 \qquad\qquad x = -2$

$\quad x = \dfrac{3}{2}$

Discard this answer, as the length of a triangle must be a positive number. ▶ State why you are discarding x = –2.

Look out for

Don't assume that an examiner will know what you're thinking – always justify why you are discarding or ignoring a result.

Example

The meerkat enclosure at a zoo is in the shape of a rectangle. It has a pathway, 1 metre wide, on 3 sides as shown below.

The length of the enclosure is $3x$ metres.

The breadth of the enclosure is one third its length.

The area of the enclosure equals the area of the path.

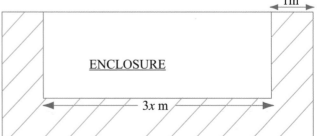

continued

Look out for

When a question asks you to 'show that', you **must** put in every line of working to explain the process. Even if it seems really obvious, still put it in!

continued

(a) Show that $3x^2 - 5x - 2 = 0$.

Solution

Area of enclosure = $3x \times x = 3x^2$
- Find the area of the enclosure.

Area of path = $(3x \times 1) + 1(x + 1) + 1(x + 1)$
= $3x + x + 1 + x + 1$
= $5x + 2$
- Find the area of the path. It can be broken down into parts in more than one way. As long as you show clearly what you are doing, it won't matter which way you do it.

Area of enclosure = Area of path
- In mathematical terms, state that the area of the enclosure is equal to the area of the path.

$3x^2 = 5x + 2$
- Substitute in the expressions for each area.

$3x^2 - 5x - 2 = 0$, as required.
- Collect all the terms on the left-hand side.
- Make sure the answer is in the same format as the question.

(b) Hence calculate the area of the enclosure.

Solution

$3x^2 - 5x - 2 = 0$

$(3x + 1)(x - 2) = 0$
- Factorise the equation – quadratic.

$3x + 1 = 0$ or $x - 2 = 0$
- Set each bracket equal to zero, and solve.

$3x = -1$ .... $x = 2$

$x = -\dfrac{1}{3}$

(Discard, as length cannot be negative)
- Discard the negative answer.

Area of enclosure = $3x^2$
- State the area of the enclosure.

= 3×2^2
- Substitute in the value of x.

= 12 m^2
- Calculate the area – remember to include the units.

Volume

You have to know the following formulae:

Volume of a Cube = l^3

Volume of a Cubiod = lbh

Volume of a Cylinder = $\pi r^2 h$

Volume of a Prism = Area of the cross-section × the height of the prism

$$= A \times h$$

The cross-section of a prism is the shape at the start and end of the prism. For example, the cross-section of a triangular prism is a triangle.

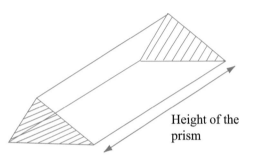

Height of the prism

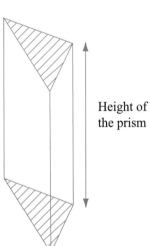

Height of the prism

Look out for

1 cm^3 = 1 ml

1000 cm^3 = 1 litre

Example

A vase, 30 centimetres high, is prism-shaped. The uniform cross-section is made up of a rectangle and a semi-circle with dimensions as shown opposite.

Find the volume of the vase.

Give your answer in litres to 2 significant figures.

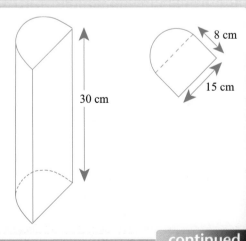

30 cm

8 cm

15 cm

continued

3

continued

Solution

Area of cross-section = Area of rectangle
+ Area of semi-circle

▶ Split the area of the cross-section into the rectangle and semi-circle.

$= lb + \frac{1}{2}\pi r^2$

$= (8 \times 15) + \left(\frac{1}{2} \times \pi \times 7.5^2 \right)$

▶ Substitute in the values to find each area.

$= 208 \cdot 357 ...$ cm^2

▶ Calculate the area of the cross-section.

Volume of vase $= 208 \cdot 357 ... \times 30$

▶ Multiply the area of the cross-section by the height of the vase.

$= 6250 \cdot 718 ...$ cm^3 ▶ Calculate the answer in cubic centimetres.

$= 6 \cdot 250 ...$ litres   ▶ Convert to litres (divide by 1000).

$= 6 \cdot 3$ litres (2 sig figs)   ▶ Round the answer sensibly, stating the degree of accuracy.

Example

A box of chocolates is in the shape of a prism, 6 centimetres high.

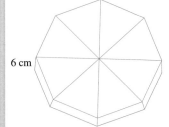
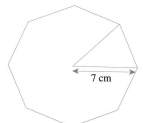

The uniform cross-section of the box is a regular octagon.
The distance from the centre of the octagon to each vertex is 7 centimetres.
Calculate the volume of the box.
Give your answer correct to three significant figures.

Solution

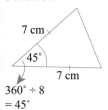

▶ Extract a triangle from the octagon.
▶ Find the angle at the centre.

$360° \div 8$
$= 45°$

Area of triangle $= \frac{1}{2} \times 7 \times 7 \sin 45°$

▶ Find the area of the triangle using $\frac{1}{2} ab\sin C°$.
See page 56 for further information.

$= 17 \cdot 324 ...$ cm^2

Area of octagon $= 17 \cdot 324 ... \times 8$

▶ Eight identical triangles make the octagon, so multiply the area of the triangle by 8.

$= 138 \cdot 592 ...$ cm^2

Volume of prism $= 138 \cdot 592 ... \times 6$

▶ Multiply the area of the octagon by the height of the box.

$= 831 \cdot 557 ...$ ▶ Evaluate the calculation.

$= 832$ cm^3 ▶ Round to 3 sig figs as asked.

Use the ANS button on your calculator to carry an answer into a new calculation. You should only ever round an answer once, and it should be in the last line of working.

Example

A tin of baked beans is in the shape of a cylinder with diameter 9 centimetres and height 14 centimetres.

The manufacturers design a new can which holds the same volume as the old can but has a reduced height of 10 centimetres.

What is the diameter of the new can?

Solution

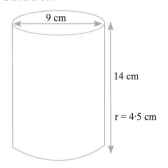

$$Vol_1 = \pi r^2 h$$ ▶ State the volume of the original can.

$$= \pi \times 4 \cdot 5^2 \times 14$$ ▶ Substitute in the values.

$$= 890 \cdot 641 \ldots \text{ cm}^3$$ ▶ Evaluate.

$$Vol_2 = \pi r^2 h$$ ▶ State the formula you will be using.

$$890 \cdot 641\ldots = \pi \times r^2 \times 10$$ ▶ Substitute in the values you know.

$$\frac{890.641\ldots}{(\pi \times 10)} = r^2$$ ▶ Rearrange to get the unknown on its own.

$$r^2 = 28 \cdot 35$$ ▶ Evaluate – remember to use a bracket on the denominator.

$$r = 5 \cdot 324\ldots$$ ▶ Square-root each side to find the radius.

$$d = 10 \cdot 648\ldots \text{ cm}$$ ▶ Double your answer to find the diameter.

$$d = 10 \cdot 6 \text{ cm (1 dp)}$$ ▶ Round sensibly, stating the degree of accuracy.

Example

A candle is in the shape of a cylinder with radius 5 centimetres and height 15 centimetres.

The candle comes in a plastic cuboid box with a square base and height 15 cm.

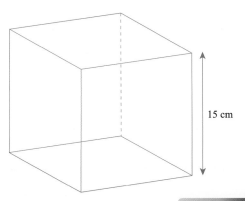

continued

3

The candle touches the inside of the cuboid at four points as shown.

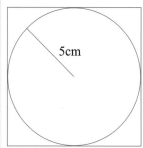

5cm

Show that the volume of the space between the candle and the cuboid is
$375(4 - \pi)$ cubic centimetres.

Solution

Volume of space = Volume of cuboid – Volume of cylinder

▶ State how to find the volume of the space.

$$= 10 \times 10 \times 15 - \pi \times 5^2 \times 15$$

▶ Substitute in values to find the two volumes.

$$= 15(10 \times 10 - \pi \times 5^2)$$

▶ Remove 15 as a common factor.

$$= 15(100 - 25\pi)$$

▶ Evaluate the bracket.

$$= 375(4 - \pi)\text{cm}^3, \text{ as required.}$$

▶ Remove 25 as a common factor.

▶ Make sure your answer is identical to the one the question gives you.

 **Look out for**

You can see that the answer has been factorised using a common factor, so try to remove a common factor as early as possible This makes the arithmetic easier and means that you are more likely to find the highest common factor.

Similarity

Shapes are mathematically similar if one is a scaled version of the other.

A scale factor of reduction is always less than 1. That is, $\dfrac{\text{small value}}{\text{large value}}$

A scale factor of enlargement is always greater than 1. That is, $\dfrac{\text{large value}}{\text{small value}}$

Look out for

The scale factor for area is (scale factor)^2.
Squared because area is two dimensional.

Look out for

The scale factor for volume is (scale factor)^3.
Cubed because volume is 3D.

Example

Carol would like a new folding table. She sees one in her local furniture store with measurements as shown below.

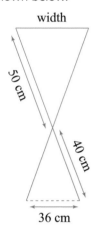

When the table is set up, two similar triangles are formed.
Carol wants a table which is at least 40 centimetres wide.
Does this table meet Carol's requirements?

SHOW ALL YOUR WORKING.

Solution

small → large ∴ scale factor of enlargement

40 cm → 50 cm   ▶ Establish whether you are reducing or enlarging.

$SF = \dfrac{50}{40} = \dfrac{5}{4}$ ▶ State the scale factor, and simplify.

Width = $\dfrac{5}{4} \times 36$ ▶ Multiply the scale factor by the width of the small triangle.

$\quad = 5 \times 9$

$\quad = 45$ cm   ▶ Calculate the width – remembering the units!

The table meets Carol's requirements,   ▶ Write a sentence to justify why the table meets
as 45 cm is more than 40 cm.   the requirements.

continued

continued

Example

Lemonade is sold in a small bottle and a large bottle
The two bottles are mathematically similar.

The large bottle is 24 cm high and contains 540 ml of lemonade.
The small bottle is 16 cm high.
Calculate how many millilitres of lemonade the small bottle contains.

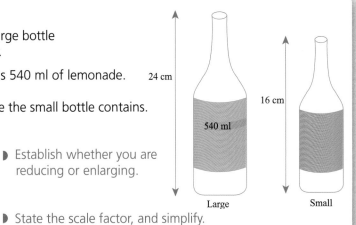

24 cm

16 cm

540 ml

Large   Small

Solution

large → small ∴ scale factor of reduction   ▶ Establish whether you are
24 cm → 16 cm   reducing or enlarging.

SF for Volume = $\left(\dfrac{16}{24}\right)^3$ ▶ State the scale factor, and simplify.
                                                    The scale factor for volume is (scale factor)^3.

$= \left(\dfrac{2}{3}\right)^3$

$= \dfrac{8}{27}$

Volume of small bottle = $\dfrac{8}{27} \times 540$ ml   ▶ Multiply the scale factor by the volume of the large bottle.

$= 160$ ml   ▶ State your answer – remembering the units!

Example

The pitch at Hampden football stadium is 69 metres wide.
A scale model of the pitch is 23 cm wide and has an area of 805 square centimetres.
What is the real length of the pitch?

Solution

small → large ∴ scale factor of enlargement

23 cm → 69 m   ▶ Establish whether you are reducing or enlarging.

SF for area = $\left(\dfrac{69}{23}\right)^2$ ▶ State the scale factor and simplify.
                                                    Scale factor for area is (scale factor)^2.

$= 9$

Area of Hampden = $9 \times 805 = 7245$ m^2 ▶ Multiply the scale factor by the area of the scale model.

Area = lb ▶ Set up an equation for the area of the real pitch.

$7245 = l \times 69$ ▶ Substitute in the values you know.

$l = \dfrac{7245}{69}$ ▶ Solve to find the length.

$l = 105$ m

The pitch is 105 m long.   ▶ State your answer clearly.

Straight line

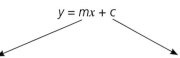

$$y = mx + c$$

▶ m is the gradient –

$$m = \frac{\text{vertical height}}{\text{horizontal distance}}$$

or $m = \dfrac{y_2 - y_1}{x_2 - x_1}$

▶ c is the y-intercept: that is, where the line cuts the y-axis.

Look out for

It doesn't matter which coordinate you make (x_1, y_1) and which you make (x_2, y_2).

For example, find the gradient of the line which passes through (2, 1) and (4, −5).

$m = \dfrac{y_2 - y_1}{x_2 - x_1}$ or $m = \dfrac{y_2 - y_1}{x_2 - x_1}$

$\quad = \dfrac{-5 - 1}{4 - 2} \qquad\qquad = \dfrac{1 - (-5)}{2 - 4}$

$\quad = \dfrac{-6}{2} \qquad\qquad\quad = \dfrac{6}{-2}$

$\quad = -3 \qquad\qquad\quad\ = -3$

Example

In the diagram below, A is the point (3, 2).

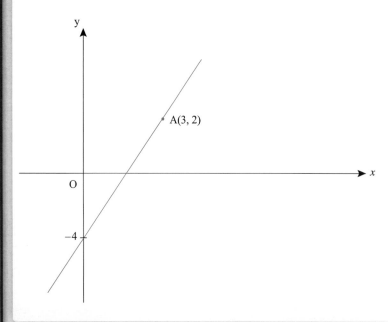

continued

continued

Solution

(a) Find the gradient of the straight line.

$(3, 2)$ $\quad m = \dfrac{y_2 - y_1}{x_2 - x_1}$ ▶ State the formula to find the gradient. You may find it helpful to
(x_1, y_1) write the coordinates at the side.

$(0, -4)$ $\quad = \dfrac{-4 - 2}{0 - 3}$ ▶ Calculate the gradient – be careful with the negative signs.
(x_2, y_2)

$\quad = \dfrac{-6}{-3}$

$\quad = 2$

(b) Hence find the equation of the straight line.

Solution

$m = 2 \quad c = -4$ ▶ State the values of m and c.

$y = mx + c$ ▶ State the general formula for a straight line.

$y = 2x - 4$ ▶ Substitute in the values of m and c.

(c) The point $(k, 4k)$ lies on the straight line.
Find the value of k.

Solution

$(k, 4k) \to x = k$ when $y = 4k$ ▶ State what you will be replacing the x and y coordinates with.

$y = 2x - 4$ ▶ Substitute in the new values.

$4k = 2k - 4$ ▶ Solve to find the value of k.

$2k = -4$

$k = -2$

Example

In an experiment involving two variables, the following values for x and y were recorded.

x	0	1	2	3	4
y	10	7	4	1	-2

The results were plotted, and a straight line was drawn through the points.
Find the gradient and write down its equation.

Solution

$(1, 7)$ $\quad m = \dfrac{y_2 - y_1}{x_2 - x_1}$ ▶ Choose any two points from the table to find the gradient. Always
(x_1, y_1) state the two points you have chosen. You will get the same
gradient regardless of which two points you use.

$(0, 10)$ $\quad = \dfrac{10 - 7}{0 - 1}$ ▶ Substitute into the gradient formula.
(x_2, y_2)

$\quad = \dfrac{3}{-1}$

$m = -3$ ▶ Calculate the gradient in its simplest form.

$c = 10$ ▶ From the table, state where the graph cuts the y-axis (it's always when x = 0)

$y = mx + c$ ▶ State the general equation of a straight line.

$y = -3x + 10$ ▶ Substitute in the values of m and c.

continued

43

Example

A tank which holds 150 litres of milk has a leak.

After 175 minutes, there is no milk left in the tank.

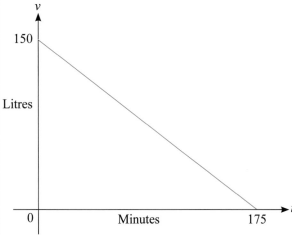

The above graph represents the volume of milk (v litres) against time (t minutes).

(a) Find the equation of the line in terms of v and t.

Solution

$(0, 150)$ $m = \dfrac{y_2 - y_1}{x_2 - x_1}$ ▶ State the two points you are going to use to find the gradient.
(x_1, y_1)

$(175, 0)$ $\quad = \dfrac{0 - 150}{175 - 0}$ ▶ Substitute into the gradient formula.
(x_2, y_2)

$\quad = -\dfrac{6}{7}$ ▶ Calculate the gradient in its simplest form.

$c = 150$ ▶ State where the graph cuts the y-axis.

$y = mx + c$ ▶ State the general equation of a straight line.

$v = mt + c$ ▶ State the general equation of a straight line in terms of t and v.

$v = -\dfrac{6}{7}t + 150$ ▶ Substitute in the values of m and c.

(b) How many minutes does it take for the container to lose 60 litres of milk?

Solution

lose = 60 litres → milk remaining = 150 − 60   ▶ Find out how much milk is remaining in
$\qquad\qquad\qquad\qquad\qquad = 90$ litres   the tank if 60 litres has been lost.

$v = -\dfrac{6}{7}t + 150$ ▶ State the equation of the line.

$90 = -\dfrac{6}{7}t + 150$ ▶ Substitute in the volume of milk remaining.

$-60 = -\dfrac{6}{7}t$ ▶ Subtract 150 from both sides.

$-420 = -6t$ ▶ Multiply both sides by 7.

$t = 70$ mins   ▶ Divide both sides by −6.

The time taken to lose 60 litres of milk is 70 minutes.   ▶ Finish by giving the answer in a sentence.

Quadratic Functions

A function of the form $f(x) = ax^2 + bx + c$, $a \neq 0$ is a quadratic function, and its graph has equation $y = ax^2 + bx + c$. A graph of this type is called a parabola. Normally, a parabola cuts the x-axis twice.

A parabola will always cut the y-axis when $x = 0$.

The points where the graph cuts the x-axis are called the **roots** of the equation.
To find the value of the roots:

▶ set the equation equal to zero: $ax^2 + bx + c = 0$

▶ factorise the equation (look for a common factor, difference of two squares or a quadratic)

▶ solve to find the values of x.

Example

The diagram below shows part of the graph of a quadratic function, with equation of the form $y = k(x - a)(x - b)$.

The graph cuts the y-axis at (0, 10) and the x-axis at (–1, 0) and (5, 0).

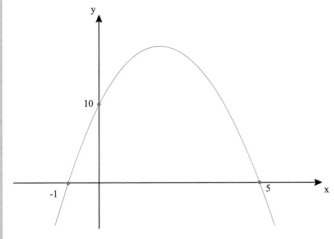

(a) Write down the values of a and b.

Solution

$x - a = 0$ or $x - b = 0$	▶	Set each bracket equal to zero.
$-1 - a = 0$ $\qquad$ $5 - b = 0$	▶	Substitute in the roots of the graph for x.
$a = -1$ $\qquad$ $b = 5$	▶	Solve to find the unknown.
$\therefore y = k(x + 1)(x - 5)$	▶	Rewrite equation with values known.

continued

(b) Calculate the value of k.

Solution

Substitute (0, 10) into the equation: ▶ State the coordinate you will be using – it should always be the y-intercept.

$y = k(x + 1)(x - 5)$

$10 = k(0 + 1)(0 - 5)$ ▶ Substitute the x and y values into the equation. The x-coordinate is the x value and the y-coordinate the y value.

$10 = k(1)(-5)$ ▶ Solve to find k.

$10 = -5k$

$k = -2$

$\therefore y = -2(x + 1)(x - 5)$ ▶ Rewrite with values known.

(c) Find the coordinates of the maximum turning point of the function.

Solution

Axis of symmetry, $x = \dfrac{-1 + 5}{2} = 2$ ▶ Find the axis of symmetry of the parabola. This can always be found by adding the roots together and dividing by 2. This tells you the x-coordinate of the turning point.

$y = -2(x + 1)(x - 5)$ ▶ State the equation you will be using.

$y = -2(2 + 1)(2 - 5)$ ▶ Substitute the x-coordinate into the equation.

$y = -2 \times 3 \times -3$ ▶ Solve to find y.

$y = 18$

$\therefore$ maximum turning point occurs at (2, 18). ▶ Give your answer as a coordinate.

Example

The diagram below shows part of the graph of $y = 4x^2 + 8x - 5$.

The graph cuts the y-axis at K and the x-axis at L and M.

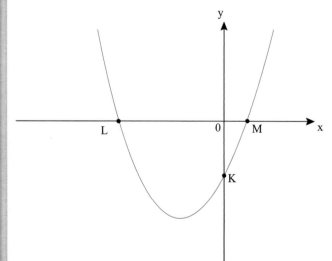

continued

(a) Write down the coordinates of K.

Solution

$y = 4x^2 + 8x - 5$

▶ K occurs when the graph cuts the y-axis – that is, when x = 0.

$y = 4(0)^2 + 8(0) - 5$

▶ Substitute x = 0 into the equation to find the y-coordinate of K. You may be able to do this by inspection rather than writing it out.

$y = -5$

$\therefore$ A(0, −5)

▶ Give your answer as a coordinate.

(b) Find the coordinates of L and M.

Solution

$4x^2 + 8x - 5 = 0$

▶ L and M are the roots of the graph (where the graph cuts the x-axis), so y = 0.

$(2x - 1)(2x + 5) = 0$

▶ Factorise the quadratic equation – you're looking for two answers!

$2x - 1 = 0$ or $2x + 5 = 0$

▶ Set each bracket equal to zero, and solve.

$2x = 1 \qquad\qquad 2x = -5$

$x = \dfrac{1}{2} \qquad\qquad x = -\dfrac{5}{2}$

$\therefore$ L $\left(-\dfrac{5}{2},\ 0\right)$ and M $\left(\dfrac{1}{2},\ 0\right)$

▶ Look at the graph to make sure that you assign the correct x-coordinate to L and M (HINT: L is negative!).

▶ Give your answer as a coordinate, stating which is L and which is M.

(c) Calculate the minimum value of $4x^2 + 8x - 5$.

Solution

Axis of symmetry, $x = \dfrac{-\dfrac{5}{2} + \dfrac{1}{2}}{2} = -\dfrac{2}{2} = -1$

▶ Find the axis of symmetry of the roots. This is the x-coordinate of the turning point.

$y = 4x^2 + 8x - 5$

$y = 4(-1)^2 + 8(-1) - 5$

▶ Substitute the value of x into the equation of the graph.

$y = 4 - 8 - 5$

▶ Calculate the value of y.

$y = -9$

$\therefore$ Minimum value occurs at −9

▶ State where the minimum value occurs.

Pythagoras' Theorem

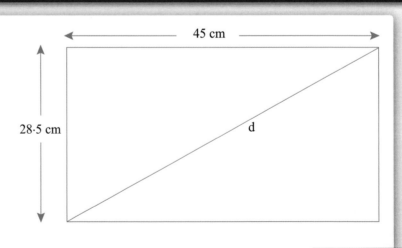

Pythagoras' Theorem states that, in any right-angled triangle, $c^2 = a^2 + b^2$

Pythagoras can be used to find:

1. the third side of a right-angled triangle when any two sides are known

2. if a triangle is right-angled when all three sides are known.

Look out for

Always justify your answer, even if the question doesn't ask you to 'give a reason for your answer'. You must still do it!

Example

Zack is making a rectangular photograph frame.

It is 45 centimetres long and 28·5 centimetres wide.

To check that the frame is rectangular, Zack measures the diagonal, *d* centimetres.

It is 55·2 centimetres long.

Has Zack made a rectangular photograph frame?

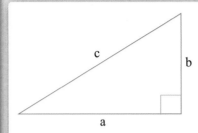

continued

continued

Solution

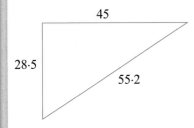

▶ Sketch the triangle.

$c^2 = a^2 + b^2$ ▶ State Pythagoras' Theorem.

$c^2 = 55{\cdot}2^2$ $a^2 + b^2 = 45^2 + 28{\cdot}5^2$ ▶ Evaluate each side individually.

   $= 3047{\cdot}04$ $= 2837{\cdot}25$

By the converse theorem of Pythagoras,
the photograph frame is not rectangular, as

$45^2 + 28{\cdot}5^2 \neq 55{\cdot}2^2$ ▶ State your conclusion – this **must** include a numerical comparison (for example, $45^2 + 28{\cdot}5^2 \neq 55{\cdot}2^2$).

Example

The diagram below shows the circular cross-section of an oil tank

It has radius 2·2 metres, and the surface of the oil is 3 metres wide.

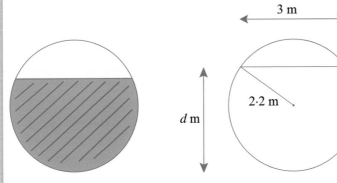

Calculate d, the depth of oil in the tank.

Solution

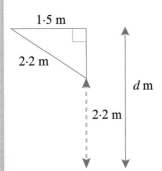

▶ A right-angled triangle is formed with the radius of the circle as the hypotenuse.

▶ 1·5 m is half of the chord length 3 m.

▶ Extract the right-angled triangle and label the sides. You can choose any letter to represent the unknown side, apart from d in this case.

continued

continued

By Pythagoras,

$c^2 = a^2 + b^2$ ▶ State Pythagoras' Theorem and substitute into it.

$2 \cdot 2^2 = 1 \cdot 5^2 + x^2$ ▶ Find the length of side x.

$x^2 = 2 \cdot 2^2 - 1 \cdot 5^2$

$x^2 = 2 \cdot 59$

$x = 1 \cdot 609 \ldots$

$\quad = 1 \cdot 6$

$d = 1 \cdot 6 + 2 \cdot 2$ ▶ The depth is the radius from the bottom of the circle to the centre plus the distance from the centre to the surface of the oil.

$\quad = 3 \cdot 8$ m

The depth of oil is 3·8 metres. ▶ State your answer.

Look out for

Always look out for radii and right-angled triangles in circle questions.

Example

The roof on a cow shed is part of a cylinder as shown in Figure 1. The roof is 7 metres wide and 2 metres high.

Figure 1

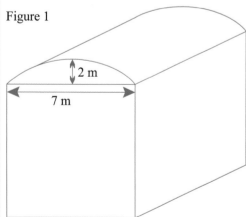

2 m

7 m

The cross-section of the shed roof is a segment on a circle with centre O, as shown in Figure 2.

continued

continued

OP is the radius of the circle.

Figure 2

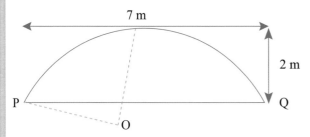

7 m

2 m

P

Q

Calculate the length of OP.

Solution

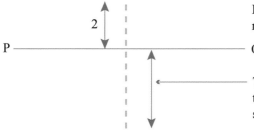

2

P ————————————— Q

Dotted line is a radius (x)

This part is the radius subtract 2.
∴ $x - 2$

3·5

x

$x - 2$ ▶ Extract the right-angled triangle and label the sides.

By Pythagoras,

$$c^2 = a^2 + b^2$$ ▶ State Pythagoras' Theorem and substitute into it.
$$x^2 = 3{\cdot}5^2 + (x - 2)^2$$

$$x^2 = 12{\cdot}25 + x^2 - 4x + 4$$ ▶ Expand the brackets.

$$x^2 = 16{\cdot}25 + x^2 - 4x$$ ▶ Simplify the right-hand side.

$16{\cdot}25 - 4x = 0$ ▶ Subtract x^2 from each side.

$$4x = 16{\cdot}25$$ ▶ Solve to find the value of x.

$$x = 4{\cdot}0625$$

$$x = 4{\cdot}1 \text{ m}$$

Length OP is 4·1 metres.   ▶ State the length of OP.

Circles

An arc is a fraction of the circumference of a circle.

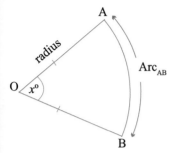

A sector is a fraction of the area of a circle.

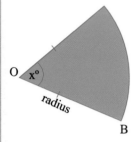

You need to know how to find the length of an arc and the area of a sector.

Length of an arc = $\dfrac{x^{\circ}}{360^{\circ}} \pi d$

Area of a sector = $\dfrac{x^{\circ}}{360^{\circ}} \pi r^2$

Example

The pendant on a necklace is a sector of a circle.

The circle has radius 27 millimetres, and the angle at the centre of the sector is 220°.

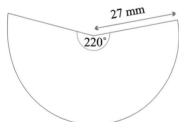

(a) Calculate the area of the pendant.

Solution

Area of pendant = $\dfrac{x^{\circ}}{360^{\circ}} \pi r^2$ ▶ State the formula for the area of a sector.

$= \dfrac{220^{\circ}}{360^{\circ}} \times \pi \times 27^2$ ▶ Substitute in the size of the angle and the radius.

$= 1399 \cdot 579 \ldots$ ▶ Evaluate and round appropriately.

$= 1400 \text{ mm}^2$

continued

continued

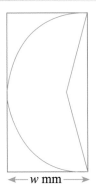

Example

(b) Each sector is cut from a rectangular piece of silver.

Find, to the nearest millimetre, the **minimum** width, w, required for the piece of silver.

← w mm →

Solution

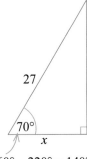

$360° − 220° = 140°$
$140° ÷ 2 = 70°$

▶ Extract the right-angled triangle, and label the sides. The triangle is formed by using the radius and a horizontal line from the centre of the circle to the side of the rectangle.

▶ Recognise right-angled trigonometry and choose the correct ratio (sin, cos or tan).

$$\cos x° = \frac{adj}{hyp}$$

$$\cos 70° = \frac{x}{27}$$

▶ Set up the equation.

$27 \cos 70° = x$

$x = 9·234 \dots$

▶ Solve to find x.

▶ Round up to the nearest mm. If you round down, you won't have enough silver!

$w = 27 + 9·234 \dots = 36·234 \dots$ mm

▶ Find the length of silver by adding the length of the radius to x.

The minimum width w can be is 37 mm

▶ State the answer.

continued

continued

Example

A wall clock has a pendulum which travels along an arc of a circle, centre C.

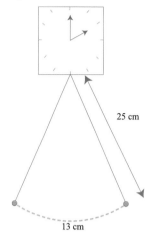 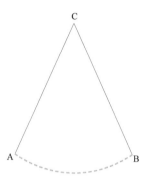

The pendulum swings from position CA to position CB.

The length of the pendulum is 25 centimetres.

The length of the arc AB is 13 centimetres.

Find the angle through which the pendulum swings from position A to position B.

Solution

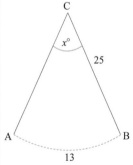

Length of arc $= \dfrac{x^\circ}{360^\circ}\pi d$	▶ State the formula for finding the length of an arc.
$13 = \dfrac{x^\circ}{360^\circ}\pi \times 50$	▶ Substitute in the values – be careful to use the diameter and not the radius.
$\dfrac{13}{(\pi \times 50)} = \dfrac{x^\circ}{360^\circ}$	▶ Divide both sides by ($\pi \times 50$). Don't evaluate it, just leave it as it is.
$\dfrac{13}{(\pi \times 50)} \times 360^\circ = x^\circ$	▶ Multiply both sides by 360.
$x^\circ = 29 \cdot 793 \ldots^\circ$	▶ Evaluate the size of the angle, and round accordingly.
$x^\circ = 30^\circ$	

continued

There are many circle facts that you need to be aware of:

▶ The angle formed in a semi–circle at the circumference is a right angle.

Note that the diameter of the circle will always be the hypotenuse of the triangle.

▶ The diameter is an axis of symmetry of the circle.

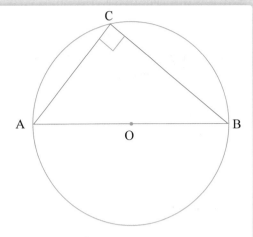

▶ When two radii are drawn to the ends of a chord, an isosceles triangle is formed.

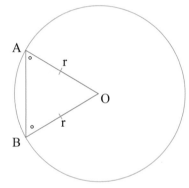

▶ A tangent is a straight line which touches a circle at only one point. A tangent and a radius make a right angle.

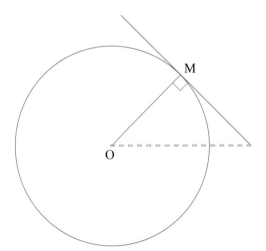

Area of a triangle; sine rule; cosine rule

You should know the three ratios for sine, cosine and tangent in a right-angled triangle:

$\sin x° = \dfrac{\text{opposite}}{\text{hypotenuse}}$

$\cos x° = \dfrac{\text{adjacent}}{\text{hypotenuse}}$

$\tan x° = \dfrac{\text{opposite}}{\text{adjacent}}$

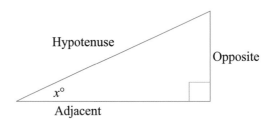

The following three formulae are given on the formula sheet at the front of the Credit paper. It is useful for you to memorise them, especially if you are planning to go on and study Higher Mathematics.

Area of a triangle $= \dfrac{1}{2}ab\sin C°$

Sine rule: $\dfrac{a}{\sin A°} = \dfrac{b}{\sin B°} = \dfrac{c}{\sin C°}$

Cosine rule: $a^2 = b^2 + c^2 - 2bc \cos A°$ or $\cos A° = \dfrac{b^2 + c^2 - a^2}{2bc}$

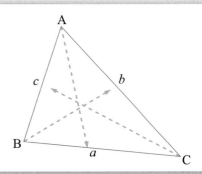

Look out for!

Capital letters are always used to represent angles or points.

Small letters are used to represent sides.

Look out for!

A side is always labelled from the angle it is across from.

You should be able to identify which formula to use for the information you are given.
This table may help with this.

What you're given	Picture	Rule
Three sides		$\cos A° = \dfrac{b^2 + c^2 - a^2}{2bc}$
Two sides and the angle between them		$a^2 = b^2 + c^2 - 2bc \cos A°$
Two sides and not the angle between them		$\dfrac{a}{\sin A°} = \dfrac{b}{\sin B°} = \dfrac{c}{\sin C°}$
One side and two angles		$\dfrac{a}{\sin A°} = \dfrac{b}{\sin B°} = \dfrac{c}{\sin C°}$

Look out for

Make sure your calculator is set in the degrees mode. It will usually appear as a D or DEG on the screen. If your calculator has G (GRAD) or R (RAD) on the screen, then it is in the wrong mode.

Example

Calculate the size of angle BAC.

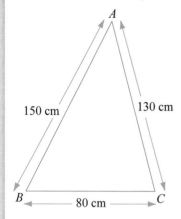

Solution

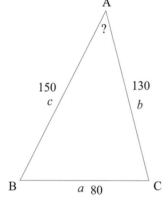

▶ Sketch the triangle and annotate with the information given.

A = ? $a = 80$
B = $b = 130$
C = $c = 150$

▶ List the sides and angles.

$$\cos A° = \frac{b^2 + c^2 - a^2}{2bc}$$

▶ State the formula (you know three sides and want to find the angle, so use the cosine rule).

$$\cos A° = \frac{130^2 + 150^2 - 80^2}{2 \times 130 \times 150}$$

▶ Substitute the values into the formula.

$$= \cos^{-1}\left(\frac{(130^2 + 150^2 - 80^2)}{(2 \times 130 \times 150)}\right)$$

▶ Show that you are finding the inverse cosine.

$= 32 \cdot 204 \ldots$

▶ Calculate your answer. Use brackets to allow you to type this into your calculator in one go.

$= 32°$

▶ Round appropriately.

∠BAC is 32°.

▶ State your answer.

continued

continued

Example

The area of triangle FGH is 29 square centimetres.

FH is 13 centimetres and GH is 8 centimetres.

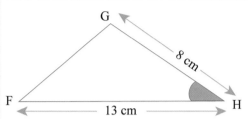

Calculate the size of the angle FHG.

Solution

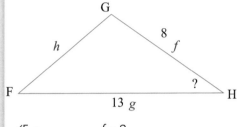

> **Look out for**
>
> Where possible, only use your calculator on the final line of working. This should avoid the chances of an inaccurate answer due to rounding errors.

$\angle F =$	$f = 8$
$\angle G =$	$g = 13$
$\angle H = ?$	$h =$

▶ Sketch the triangle – annotate with the information given.

▶ List the sides and angles.

$$A_\Delta = \frac{1}{2} fg \sin H°$$

▶ State the formula for the area of the triangle.

$$29 = \frac{1}{2} 8 \times 13 \times \sin H°$$

▶ Substitute in the values given.

$$\frac{29}{\frac{1}{2} \times 8 \times 13} = \sin H°$$

▶ Divide both sides by $\frac{1}{2} \times 8 \times 13$. There's no need to evaluate this.

$$H° = \sin^{-1}\left(\frac{29}{\left(\frac{1}{2} \times 8 \times 13\right)}\right)$$

▶ Find the inverse sine of $\left(\frac{29}{\left(\frac{1}{2} \times 8 \times 13\right)}\right)$.

Remember to include the bracket around $\frac{29}{\left(\frac{1}{2} \times 8 \times 13\right)}$ when you type it into your calculator.

$$= 33·896 \ldots$$

$$= 34°$$

▶ Round the angle appropriately.

$\therefore$ angle FHG is 34°.

▶ State the answer.

Example

In triangle ABC,

AB = 3 units
AC = 6 units
BC = 5 units.

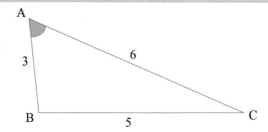

Show that $\cos A° = \dfrac{5}{12}$

Solution

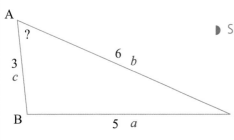

▶ Sketch the triangle – annotate with the information given.

$\angle A = ?$	$a = 5$
$\angle B =$	$b = 6$
$\angle C =$	$c = 3$

▶ List the sides and the angles.

$$\cos A° = \frac{b^2 + c^2 - a^2}{2bc}$$

▶ State the formula.

$$\cos A° = \frac{6^2 + 3^2 - 5^2}{2 \times 6 \times 3}$$

▶ Substitute in the values known.

$$= \frac{36 + 9 - 25}{36}$$

▶ Evaluate the numerator and denominator.

$$= \frac{20}{36}$$

$$\cos A° = \frac{5}{12} \quad \text{as required.}$$

▶ Simplify to get the answer.

Look out for

If you don't get the same answer as the one given, then you've made a mistake somewhere.

An angle of **elevation** is the angle between the horizontal and your line of sight when you are looking **up** at an object.

An angle of **depression** is the angle between the horizontal and your line of sight when you are looking **down** at an object.

Look out for

If you are told two angles in the triangle, always work out the third angle. Remember that the three angles in the triangle add up to 180°.

Example

A rescue helicopter, at point H, hovers between a lifeboat, L, and a ship, S.

The helicopter is 820 metres from the lifeboat.

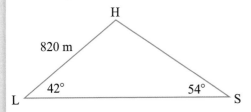

From the lifeboat, the angle of elevation of the helicopter is 42°.
From the ship, the angle of elevation of the helicopter is 54°.
Calculate the distance from the lifeboat to the ship.

Solution

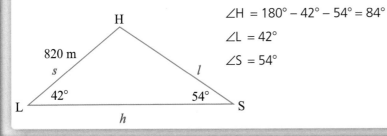

$\angle H = 180° - 42° - 54° = 84°$ $\quad h = ?$
$\angle L = 42°$ $\quad l =$
$\angle S = 54°$ $\quad s = 740$

▶ Sketch and annotate the triangle.
▶ List the sides and angles.

continued

continued

$$\frac{h}{\sin H°} = \frac{s}{\sin S°}$$

▶ We want to find a side, and we know three angles and one side.

▶ We must use the sine rule.

▶ We only need to state the two parts of the sine rule we intend to use

$$\frac{h}{\sin 84°} = \frac{820}{\sin 54°}$$

▶ Substitute the values into the formula.

$$h = \frac{820 \sin 84°}{\sin 54°}$$

▶ Multiply both sides by sin 84°.

$$=1008{\cdot}023 \ldots$$

▶ Calculate h.

$$= 1008 \text{ metres}$$

▶ Round appropriately.

The lifeboat and the ship are 1008 metres apart. ▶ State the answer.

Look out for !

You may need to use Pythagoras or right-angled trigonometry as part of a question when you are asked to find a length or a height which isn't the side of the triangle.

Example

Judith is walking along a clifftop path when she notices a sailing boat in the sea below her.

Ian is walking along the same path, 670 metres ahead of Judith. He also notices the sailing boat.

The angle of depression from Judith to the sailing boat is 52°.

The angle of depression from Ian to the sailing boat is 65°.

How high above sea level is the cliff?

continued

continued

Solution

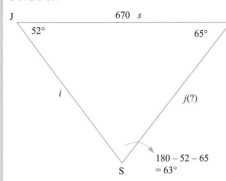

▶ Sketch the triangle and annotate with the information told.

▶ Calculate the third angle of the triangle – include this in the sketch.

$180 - 52 - 65$
$= 63°$

$\angle J = 52°$ $j = ?$
$\angle I = 65°$ $i =$
$\angle S = 63°$ $s = 670$

▶ List the sides and angles.

$$\frac{j}{\sin J°} = \frac{s}{\sin S°}$$

▶ State the formula. (You know three angles and one side, so use the sine rule).

$$\frac{j}{\sin 52°} = \frac{670}{\sin 63°}$$

▶ Substitute in the values known. At this point, you can find either side j or side i. Both are equally correct and valid strategies.

$$j = \frac{670 \sin 52°}{\sin 63°}$$

▶ Rearrange to find side j.

$j = 592{\cdot}551 \ldots$

▶ Calculate side j.

$= 593$ metres

▶ Round appropriately.

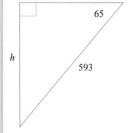

▶ Sketch a right-angled triangle to find the height of the cliff.
▶ Annotate with the information known.
▶ Label the side you are trying to find.
▶ If you have chosen to find side i, this sketch will be different.

$$\sin x° = \frac{\text{opp}}{\text{hyp}}$$

▶ State the formula.

$$\sin 65° = \frac{h}{593}$$

▶ Substitute in the values.

$593 \sin 65° = h$

▶ Rearrange to find side h.

$h = 537{\cdot}440 \ldots$

▶ Calculate side h.

$= 537$ metres

▶ Round appropriately.

The cliff is 537 metres above sea-level.

▶ State the answer.

Bearings

Reminder

Corresponding Angles

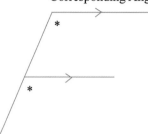

Vertically Opposite Angles

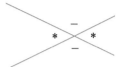

Alternate Angles

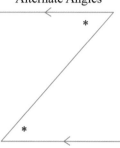

A bearing is the size of angle measured in a clockwise direction from the north line.

Look out for !

Due east means a bearing of 090°.

Due south means a bearing of 180°.

Due west means a bearing of 270°.

Look out for !

You must always draw a clearly labelled diagram and show all working regardless of how easy you think it is!

Example

Two ships leave from the harbour, H.

The *Albatross* sails on a bearing of 063° for 140 kilometres and stops.

The *Guillemot* sails on a bearing of 150° for 270 kilometres and stops.

How far apart are the two boats when they have both stopped?

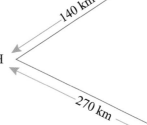

Solution

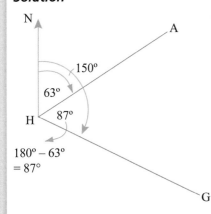

$180° - 63°$
$= 87°$

▶ Sketch the diagram, adding in north lines where appropriate. Annotate with the information known.

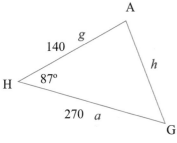

▶ Sketch the triangle.

$\angle H = 87°$ $h = ?$

$\angle A =$ $a = 270$

$\angle G =$ $g = 140$

▶ List the values.

$$h^2 = a^2 + g^2 - 2ag \cos H°$$

▶ State the formula (two sides and the angle between them are known, so use the cosine rule).

$$h^2 = 270^2 + 140^2 - 2 \times 270 \times 140 \times \cos 87°$$

▶ Substitute into the formula.

$$= 88\,543{\cdot}401\ldots$$

▶ Evaluate the right-hand side. This can be done in one line on your calculator.

$$h = 297{\cdot}562\ldots$$

▶ Square-root both sides of the equation.

$$= 298 \text{ km}$$

▶ Round appropriately.

The two ships are 298 km apart.

▶ State the answer.

Example

Three friends, Robina (R), Isabel (I) and Brian (B), live in the same town.

Robina lives 3 kilometres due south of Isabel.

Isabel lives 5·5 kilometres from Brian.

Brian is on a bearing of 140° from Robina.

Calculate the bearing of Brian from Isabel.

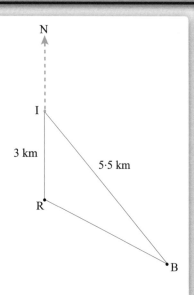

Solution

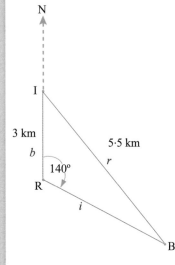

▶ Make a sketch of the diagram, annotating with the information known.

▶ Sketch the triangle.

$\angle R = 140°$ $r = 5·5$

$\angle I =$ $i =$

$\angle B = ?$ $b = 3$

▶ List the values.

$$\frac{r}{\sin R°} = \frac{b}{\sin B°}$$

▶ State the formula (two sides and one other angle is sine rule).

$$\frac{5·5}{\sin 140°} = \frac{3}{\sin B°}$$

▶ Substitute into the formula.

$5·5 \sin B° = 3 \sin 140°$

▶ Cross-multiply by each denominator.

$$\sin B° = \frac{3 \sin 140°}{5·5}$$

▶ Divide both sides by 5·5.

$$B° = \sin^{-1}\left(\frac{3\sin 140°}{5·5}\right)$$

▶ Find the inverse sine.

$= 20·524 …$

▶ Evaluate the answer.

$B = 21°$

▶ Round appropriately.

▶ Sketch the triangle to fill in the new values known.

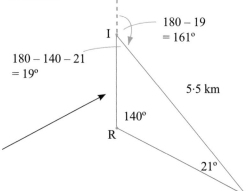

∴ the bearing of Brian from Isabel is 161°.

▶ State the answer.

Example

Two hotels are within walking distance of a local tourist attraction.

From Hotel A, the tourist attraction, T, is on a bearing of 076°.

From Hotel B, the tourist attraction is on a bearing of 320°.

(a) Calculate the size of angle ATB.

Solution

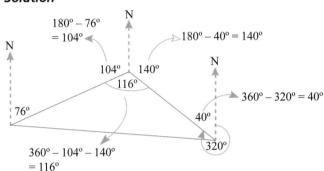

- Sketch the diagram, adding in north lines where appropriate.
- Find the acute angle at B.
- Use alternate angles to find the size of the angles at point T.
- State the answer.

$\therefore \angle$ATB is 116°.

(b)

The tourist attraction is 240 metres from Hotel A and is 130 metres from Hotel B.

Calculate the direct distance from Hotel A to Hotel B.

Solution

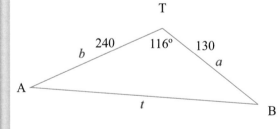

- Sketch the triangle and annotate with the information known.

$\angle A =$ $a = 130$

$\angle T = 116°$ $t = ?$

$\angle B =$ $b = 240$

- List the values.

$t^2 = a^2 + b^2 - 2ab \cos T°$

- State the formula (two sides and the angle between them is the cosine rule).

$t^2 = 130^2 + 240^2 - 2 \times 130 \times 240 \cos 116°$

- Substitute into the formula.

$\quad = 101\,854{\cdot}359 \ldots$

- Evaluate the right-hand side.

$t = 319{\cdot}146 \ldots$

- Square-root both sides.

$\quad = 319$ metres

- Round appropriately.

The distance between Hotel A and Hotel B is 319 metres.

- State the answer.

Trigonometric Graphs

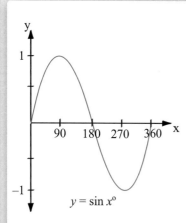

$y = \sin x^\circ$

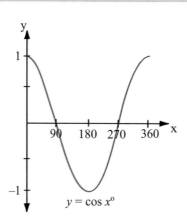

$y = \cos x^\circ$

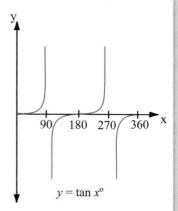

$y = \tan x^\circ$

One full cycle of a sine graph occurs within $360^\circ \rightarrow 0 \le x \le 360$.

One full cycle of a cosine graph occurs within $360^\circ \rightarrow 0 \le x \le 360$.

One full cycle of a tangent graph occurs within $180^\circ \rightarrow 0 \le x \le 180$.

The maximum value of the sine and cosine graphs is 1.

The minimum value of the sine and cosine graphs is –1.

The tangent graph has an undefined maximum and minimum value.

$y = a \sin bx^\circ$ $\qquad\qquad\qquad$ $y = a \cos bx^\circ$

a is the amplitude. The amplitude of the graph is $\dfrac{\text{maximum} - \text{minimum}}{2}$.

b is the period of the graph. The period of the graph is $\dfrac{360^\circ}{b}$.

$y = \tan bx^\circ$

The period of a tangent graph is $\dfrac{180^\circ}{b}$.

The amplitude of a tangent graph cannot be measured.

Example

The graph of $y = a \cos bx^\circ$,
$0 \le x \le 120$, is shown opposite.

State the equation of the graph in the
form $y = a \cos bx^\circ$

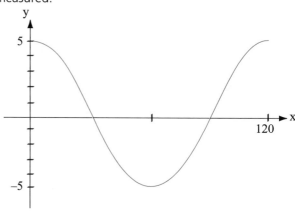

continued

continued

Solution

$$a = \frac{5-(-5)}{2} = \frac{10}{2} = 5$$

$$b = \frac{360°}{120°} = 3$$

$$\therefore y = 5 \cos 3x°$$

Example

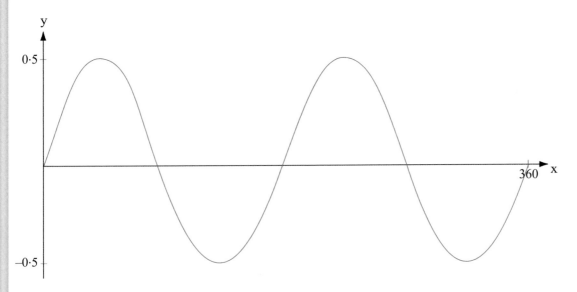

The diagram shows the graph of $y = p \sin qx°$, $0 \le x \le 360$.

Find the values of p and q.

Solution

$$p = \frac{0 \cdot 5 - (-0 \cdot 5)}{2} = \frac{1}{2}$$

There are two full cycles of the graph within 360°.

$$\therefore q = 2$$

Trigonometric Equations

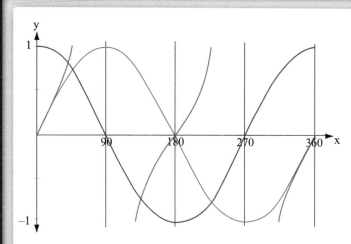

From the diagram, above we can see the following:

1. All three graphs are positive (that is, above the x-axis) between 0° and 90°.

2. Only the sine graph is positive between 90° and 180°.

3. Only the tangent graph is positive between 180° and 270°.

4. Only the cosine graph is positive between 270° and 360°.

Using this information gives us the four quadrants for All, Sine, Tan, Cos (you may know it as a CAST diagram).

Sin $180 - x$	All x
Tan $180 + x$	Cos $360 - x$

A trig equation should usually give rise to two solutions. We use the quadrants to work out when the graph is positive.

Example

Solve algebraically the equation $\sqrt{2}\sin x° + 1 = 0$ $\qquad$ $0 \le x \le 360$.

Solution

$\sqrt{2}\sin x° + 1 = 0$

$\qquad \sqrt{2}\sin x° = -1$

$\qquad\quad \sin x° = -\dfrac{1}{\sqrt{2}}$

▶ Rearrange the equation to get $\sin x°$ on its own.

× S	× A
✓ T	C ✓

▶ $\sin x°$ is equal to a negative number, therefore it is not positive in the All or Sine quadrants. This means it must have solutions in the Tan and Cos quadrants instead.

continued

continued

Acute angle = $\sin^{-1}\left(\dfrac{1}{\sqrt{2}}\right)$ = 45°   ▶ Find the acute angle that you will be working with.

$x°$ = 180 + 45, 360 − 45   ▶ State the values you are going to find.

$x°$ = 225°, 315°   ▶ State the answers.

Example

The diagram below shows part of the graph of $y = \cos x°$.

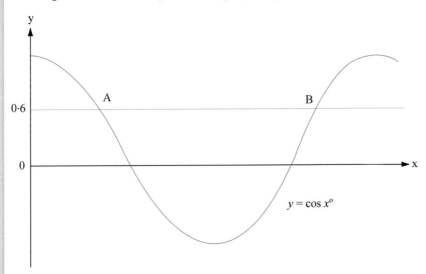

The line $y = 0·6$ is drawn and cuts the graph of $y = \cos x°$ at A and B.

Find the coordinates of A and B.

Solution

$\cos x° = 0·6$

▶ The graphs of $\cos x°$ and 0·6 are equal to each other at points A and B. Write this in mathematical language.

▶ $\cos x°$ is equal to a positive number, so the solutions occur in the All and Cos quadrants.

Acute angle = $\cos^{-1}(0·6)$ = 53·1°   ▶ Find the acute angle that you will be working with.

$x°$ = 53·1°, 360 − 53·1°   ▶ State the values you are going to find.

= 53·1°, 306·9°   ▶ Calculate these values.

∴ A is the point (53·1, 0·6) and B is the point (306·9, 0·6).   ▶ State the answer in coordinate form as asked in the question.

continued

Example

The depth of water, D metres, in a harbour on a certain day, t hours after midnight, is given by the formula

$D = 7 + 4.5 \sin (30t)°$.

(a) State the maximum value of D.

Solution

Maximum of $D = 7 + 4.5 = 11.5$ metres.   ▶ The maximum point on $4.5 \sin (30t)°$ is 4.5.
                                             $7 + 4.5 \sin (30t)°$ increases the maximum value by 7.

(b) Find the depth of the water at 2:30pm.

Solution

2:30pm is 14·5 hours on from midnight   ▶ Convert 2:30pm into the numbers of hours after
$\rightarrow t = 14.5$ midnight.

$D = 7 + 4.5 \sin (30t)$ ▶ State the equation.

$\quad = 7 + 4.5 \sin (30 \times 14.5)$ ▶ Substitute $t = 14.5$ into the equation.

$\quad = 11.346 \ldots$ ▶ Evaluate the right-hand side.

$\quad = 11.3$ metres   ▶ Round appropriately.

The depth of water at 2:30pm is 11·3 metres.

(c) When is the depth of the water first 9·25 metres?

Solution

$7 + 4.5 \sin (30t) = D$ ▶ State the equation.

$7 + 4.5 \sin (30t) = 9.25$ ▶ $D = 9.25$ when the depth is 9·25 metres.
                                          ▶ State the equation.
                                          ▶ Substitute $D = 9.25$ into the equation.

$4.5 \sin (30t)° = 2.25$ ▶ Subtract 7 from both sides.

$\sin (30t) = \dfrac{2.25}{4.5}$ ▶ Divide both sides by 4·5.

$30t = \sin^{-1}\left(\dfrac{2.25}{4.5}\right)$ ▶ Find the inverse sine. As we only need the first time it
                                          is 9·25, we don't need to look at the other quadrants.

$30t = 30$ ▶ Divide both sides by 30.

$t = 1$ ▶ The number of hours after midnight is 1.

midnight + 1 hour = 1am   ▶ State the answer. Be sure to state an exact time,
$\therefore$ the first time the water is 9·25 metres   including am or pm as appropriate. You could also
deep is at 1am.   give the time in 24-hour clock (e.g. 0100).

Trigonometric identities

$\tan x° = \dfrac{\sin x°}{\cos x°}$

$\sin^2 x° + \cos^2 x° = 1 \rightarrow$ $\qquad \therefore \sin^2 x° = 1 - \cos^2 x°$

$\qquad\qquad\qquad\qquad\qquad$ and $\cos^2 x° = 1 - \sin^2 x°$

The formulae above are very seldom assessed at Credit level. However, they are still part of the Credit course. They need to be memorised, as they are not given on the formula sheet. If you are planning to study Higher Mathematics, then it is essential that you know these formulae.

Example

Prove that $\cos^3 x° + \cos x° \sin^2 x° = \cos x°$.

Solution

$\cos^3 x° + \cos x° \sin^2 x°$
▶ State the left-hand side of the equation. When you are asked to 'prove that …', you need to show all the lines that take you from the left-hand side to the right-hand side.

$= \cos x° (\cos^2 x° + \sin^2 x°)$
▶ Remove a common factor of $\cos x°$.

$= \cos x° (1)$
▶ Use the fact that $\cos^2 x° + \sin^2 x = 1$.

$= \cos x°$, as required.
▶ Simplify to achieve the answer.

Example

Solve $\sin x° - 2\cos x° = 0$, for $0 \le x \le 360$.

Solution

$\sin x° - 2\cos x° = 0$
▶ State the equation.

$\qquad \sin x° = 2\cos x°$
▶ Add $2\cos x°$ to each side.

$\qquad \dfrac{\sin x°}{\cos x°} = 2$
▶ Divide each side by $\cos x°$.

$\qquad \tan x° = 2$
▶ Use the fact that $\dfrac{\sin x°}{\cos x°} = \tan x°$.

$\qquad$ Acute angle $= \tan^{-1}(2) = 63\cdot4°$
▶ Find the acute angle you'll be working with.

▶ $\tan x°$ is equal to a positive number, so it will be positive in the All and Tan quadrants.

$$
\begin{array}{c|c}
\overset{\times}{\text{S}} & \text{A}\;\checkmark \\
\hline
\checkmark\;\text{T} & \text{C}^{\times}
\end{array}
$$

$\qquad x° = 63\cdot4,\ 180 + 63\cdot4$
▶ Show the values you are going to find.

$\qquad x° = 63\cdot4°,\ 243\cdot4°$
▶ State the answer.

The Averages

Reminders

Mean: $\bar{x} = \dfrac{\text{sum of the values}}{\text{the number of values}}$

Look out for

$\bar{x}$ is the symbol for the mean.

The **Mode** is the most common (frequent) value. Remember that there can be more than one modal value.

The **Median** is the middle value in an ordered set of data.

▶ When there are an odd number of values, the median is the middle number.

For example:

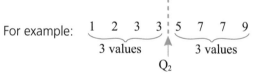

median = 6

▶ When there are an even number of values, the median is the mean of the two values either side of the halfway lines

For example: 1   2   3   3 ┊ 5   7   7   9
           3 values   3 values
                 Q_2

median $= \dfrac{3+5}{2} = 4$

Look out for

Q_2 is the symbol for the median.

Look out for

Q_1 is the symbol for the lower quartile.

The **Lower Quartile** is the median of the lower half of the data.

For example: 1   2 ┊ 3   3 ┊ 5   7   7   9
                 Q_1 Q_2

lower quartile $= \dfrac{2+3}{2} = 2 \cdot 5$

The **Upper Quartile** is the median of the upper half of the data.

For example: 1   2   3   3 ┊ 5   7 ┊ 7   9   upper quartile $= \dfrac{7+7}{2} = 7$
                    Q_2 Q_3

Look out for

Q_3 is the symbol for the upper quartile.

Measures of spread

Reminders

The **Range** = Highest Value – Lowest Value

The Interquartile Range: $\qquad IQR = Q_3 - Q_1$

The Semi-Interquartile Range: $\quad SIQR = \dfrac{Q_3 - Q_1}{2}$

Standard Deviation $\qquad\qquad s = \sqrt{\dfrac{\sum(x-\bar{x})^2}{n-1}} = \sqrt{\dfrac{\sum x^2 - \dfrac{(\sum x)^2}{n}}{n-1}}$

Look out for

$\sum$ is the symbol for 'the sum of' – that is, all the values added together.

▶ When the mean is used for the average, then we use the standard deviation to look at the spread of the data.

▶ When the median is used for the average, then we use the quartiles and the range to look at the spread of the data.

Five-figure summary

It's often useful to summarise large amounts of data by looking at the five-figure summary.

The five numbers are:
▶ the lowest value (L)
▶ the highest value (H)
▶ the lower quartile (Q_1)
▶ the median (Q_2)
▶ the upper quartile (Q_3).

Example

(a) The temperature, in degrees Celsius, in Belfast over a two–week period in January was recorded and is shown below.

1·5   2·7   4·4   7·9   9·2   4·9   10·6   6·3   9·7   9·5   5·0   3·7   9·4   8·8

Find the five-figure summary for this data.

Solution

| 1·5 | 2·7 | 3·7 | (4·4) | 4·9 | 5·0 | 6·3 | 7·9 | 8·8 | 9·2 | (9·4) | 9·5 | 9·7 | 10·6 |

$Q_2 = \dfrac{6\cdot3 + 7\cdot9}{2} = 7\cdot1$

L = 1·5
$Q_1 = 4\cdot4$
$Q_2 = 7\cdot1$
$Q_3 = 9\cdot4$
H = 10·6

▶ Put the temperatures into ascending numerical order.
▶ State the lowest and highest values.
▶ Find the median (Q_2).
▶ Find the lower quartile (Q_1). This is the median of the first seven values (that is, the fourth value).
▶ Find the upper quartile (Q_3). This is the median of the second seven values (that is, the eleventh value).
▶ State the five-figure summary.

(b) Find   (i) the interquartile range
          (ii) the semi-interquartile range.

Solution

(i) IQR = 9·4 − 4·4 = 5

(ii) SIQR = $\dfrac{9\cdot4 - 4\cdot4}{2} = \dfrac{5}{2} = 2\cdot5$

Statistical diagrams

At Credit level, you are sometimes given data and asked to draw 'an appropriate statistical diagram'. If this is the case, you should be considering drawing a box plot, a stem-and-leaf diagram or a dot plot.

Box plots

The values calculated in the five–figure summary can be displayed in a box plot. The diagram clearly shows the quartiles (the box), the median (the line inside the box) and the lowest and highest values (the whiskers).

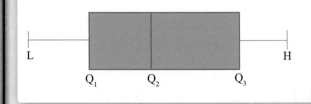

Look out for !

Looking at the diagram opposite, you can see that:

▶ the first 25% of the data lies between L and Q_1
▶ the first 50% of the data lies between L and Q_2
▶ the first 75% of the data lies between L and Q_3
▶ the middle 50% of the data lies between Q_1 and Q_3
▶ the upper 25% of the data lies between Q_3 and H.

Example

(a) The weights, in kilogrammes, of the players in two rugby teams are shown below.

Team A					Team B				
79	85	89	93	100	83	85	91	95	95
102	104	105	105	105	96	102	103	104	107
105	106	107	117	126	107	108	109	112	115

On the same diagram, draw a box plot to illustrate the distribution of weights for each team.

Solution

79	85	89	(93)	100
102	104	(105)	105	105
105	(106)	107	117	125

Team A
L = 79 kg
Q_1 = 93 kg
Q_2 = 105 kg
Q_3 = 106 kg
H = 126 kg

▶ Starting with Team A, check that the data is in numerical order. If not, order it.
▶ State the lowest and highest values.
▶ Find the median (fifteen values in total, so the eighth value).
▶ Find the lower quartile (seven values in the lower quartile, so the fourth value).
▶ Find the upper quartile (seven values in the upper quartile, so the twelfth value).

83	83	91	(95)	95
96	102	(103)	104	107
107	(108)	109	112	115

Team B
L = 83 kg
Q_1 = 95 kg
Q_2 = 103 kg
Q_3 = 108 kg
H = 115 kg

▶ Now look at the values for Team B. Check that the data is in numerical order. If not, order it.
▶ State the lowest and highest values.
▶ Find the median (15 values in total, so the 8th value).
▶ Find the lower quartile (7 values in the lower quartile, so the 4th value).
▶ Find the upper quartile (7 values in the upper quartile, so the 12th value).

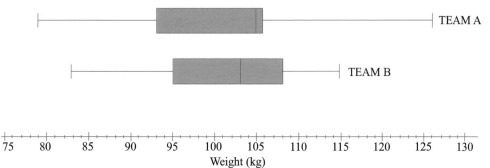

Weights of rugby teams

▶ Draw an appropriate scale – the lowest weight is 79 and the highest is 126.
▶ Label the x-axis.
▶ Mark on the values from the five-figure summary for Team A and then draw the box plot.
▶ Mark on the values from the five-figure summary for Team B and then draw the box plot.
▶ Remember to give the diagram a heading.

(b) Compare the two rugby teams, and comment.

Solution

The median of Team A is higher than that of Team B, so Team A tends to be the heavier team.

▶ Look at the medians for each team. Team A has a higher median than Team B, which means that Team A is typically the heavier team.

However, the weight of Team B is less varied and more consistent, as it has a lower range than Team A.

▶ Look at the spread of the box plots. Team A has a range of 47 whereas Team B has a range of 32. This means that Team B's weights are closer together.

Look out for

If you are asked to compare or comment on data, then you need to put it into the context of the question. It is not enough to just quote figures – you need to say what this means.

Stem-and-leaf diagrams

Stem-and-leaf diagrams are another way of displaying data.

Example

(a) Using the same data as before, draw a back-to-back stem-and-leaf diagram to illustrate the weight of the two rugby teams.

Solution

TEAM A   TEAM B

9	7	
9 5	8	3 5
3	9	1 5 5 6
7 6 5 5 5 5 4 2	10	2 3 4 7 7 8 9
7	11	2 5
6	12	

7/11 represents 117 kg   8/3 represents 83 kg

$n = 15$ $n = 15$

continued

Look out for

When the data is already ordered, remember to count along in the direction it is increasing to find the quartiles and median (in the example above, from left to right).

Stem-and-leaf diagrams – continued

- Make the stem of the diagram – look at the lowest and highest values for both teams to decide on the first and last value of the stem.
- It doesn't matter what side you put Team A and Team B on as long as you clearly label each side.
- Starting with one of the teams, go through the data, adding it to the correct level. Try to be systematic – go through it either row by row OR column by column. Since the data given in this question is in numerical order along the rows, enter the data row by row.
- Now enter the data for the other team on the opposite side of the diagram.
- Once you have finished the diagram, count the number of entries and make sure it matches the number of pieces of data in the question (15 entries on each side of the diagram).
- If the stem-and-leaf diagram isn't in numerical order, draw another diagram and make it ordered.
- Give the diagram a heading.
- State how many pieces of data are in the diagram ($n = 15$).
- Remember to include a key to explain how to read the information on each side of diagram.

(b) State the median, lower and upper quartiles for this data.

Solution

```
              TEAM A                              TEAM B

                          9 │  7 │
                        9 5 │  8 │ 3  5
                        (3) │  9 │ 1 (5) 5  6
    7 (6) 5 5 5 (5) 4  2 │ 10 │ 2 (3) 4  7  7 (8)  9
                        7 │ 11 │ 2  5
                        6 │ 12 │
```

7/11 represents 117 kg   8/3 represents 83 kg

$n = 15$ $n = 15$

> **Look out for**
>
> The leaves are ordered from the stem outwards on both sides of the diagram.

Team A	Team B
$Q_1 = 93$ kg	$Q_1 = 95$ kg
$Q_2 = 105$ kg	$Q_2 = 103$ kg
$Q_3 = 106$ kg	$Q_3 = 108$ kg

- The median is the 8th value.
- The lower quartile is the 4th value.
- The upper quartile is the 12th value.

> **Look out for**
>
> When locating Q_1, Q_2 and Q_3 on the diagram, remember to include the stem as well as the leaf,
> eg Median of Team A is 105 kg not 5 kg.

> **Look out for**
>
> Remember to count from right to left to find the median and quartiles on the left-hand side of the diagram – that is, Team A in the stem-and-leaf diagram above.

Dot plots

A dot plot is yet another way of graphing data. As the name suggests, it is a graph that uses dots, and it quickly shows the distribution of the graph.

Distributions:

skewed to the right

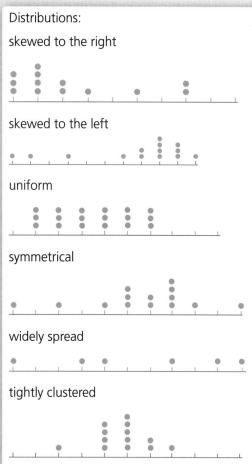

skewed to the left

uniform

symmetrical

widely spread

tightly clustered

Each dot represents one piece of data, and there can't be any data in between the numbers on the scale.

continued

Dot plots – continued

Example

Twenty people were asked how many pieces of fruit and vegetables they ate in a day.

4   5   4   5   3   4   2   4   6   6
5   5   6   5   5   5   1   4   5   3

Solution

(a) Construct a dot plot for the data.

Number of pieces of fruit and veg eaten

▶ Find the lowest and highest values and choose an appropriate scale.
▶ Place a dot above the appropriate number on the scale for each value given.
▶ Check that you have 20 dots for 20 pieces of data.

(b) What is the modal value?

Solution

Mode = 5

▶ The mode is the value with the most dots above it. It should be easy to spot!

(c) Describe the shape of the distribution.

Solution

The distribution is skewed to the left.

Frequency tables

A frequency table is an efficient way to organise and order data when several values occur repeatedly. The mean can very easily be determined from a frequency table.

Example

A carton of orange juice is advertised as containing 1000 millilitres. To monitor quality control, several cartons were opened and the volume of liquid measured.

Volume (ml) (x)	Frequency (f)	$f \times x$
997	7	
998	9	
999	4	
1000	12	
1001	8	
1002	4	
1003	6	
TOTAL		

Use the table above to calculate the mean volume of a carton of orange juice.

Solution

Volume (ml) (x)	Frequency (f)	$x \times f$
997	7	$997 \times 7 = 6979$
998	9	$998 \times 9 = 8982$
999	4	$999 \times 4 = 3996$
1000	12	$1000 \times 12 = 12\,000$
1001	8	$1001 \times 8 = 8008$
1002	4	$1002 \times 4 = 4008$
1003	6	$1003 \times 6 = 6018$
TOTAL	50	49991

$$\bar{x} = \frac{49991}{50} = 999 \cdot 82 \text{ cm}^3$$

▶ Add up all the frequencies to total the frequency column.

▶ Multiply the volume by the frequency to fill in the last column. You don't need to write the parts in green, but please put them in if it helps.

▶ Total the end column.

▶ The mean is the total of the frequency column divided by the total of the $f \times x$ column.

Cumulative frequency

The cumulative frequency is the running total on a frequency table. It can then be used to find the median and quartiles of the data.

Example

The number of goals being scored by teams in a Sunday football league was recorded.

No. of Goals	Frequency	Cumulative Frequency
0	9	
1	10	
2	6	
3	5	
4	3	
5	8	
6	4	

Solution

(a) Complete the cumulative frequency column.

No. of Goals	Frequency	Cumulative Frequency
0	9	9
1	10	9 + 10 = 19
2	6	19 + 6 = 25
3	5	25 + 5 = 30
4	3	30 + 3 = 33
5	8	33 + 8 = 41
6	4	41 + 4 = 45

▶ Add the previous frequency to the total frequencies each time. It is not necessary to show the part in green but if it helps feel free to put it in.

(b) Calculate the median and quartiles for this data.

Solution

No. of Goals	Frequency	Cumulative Frequency	
0	9	9	1st to 9th values
1	10	19	10th to 19th values
2	6	25	20th to 25th values
3	5	30	26th to 30th values
4	3	33	31st to 33rd values
5	8	41	34th to 41st values
6	4	45	42nd to 45th values

▶ You may find it useful to add the text in green to help you understand how to find the median and quartiles from the cumulative frequency.

continued

Median = 2 goals

▶ 45 values, so the median is the 23rd value ($\frac{45+1}{2}$ = 23rd value).

▶ The 23rd value occurs between the 20th and 25th values on the table, so the median is 2 goals.

Lower quartile = 1 goal

▶ 22 values in the lower quartile. Median of the lower quartile occurs between the 11th and 12th values.

▶ The 11th and 12th values occur between the 10th and 19th values on the table, so the lower quartile is 1 goal.

Upper quartile = 5 goals

▶ 22 values in the upper quartile. Median of the upper quartile occurs between the 34th and 35th values (23 + 11 and 23 + 12).

▶ The 34th and 35th values occur between the 34th and 41st values on the table, so the upper quartile is 5 goals.

Scatter Diagrams and Line of Best Fit

A scatter diagram is used to graph two sets of data to see if there is a connection between them. The connection between the data is known as the correlation.

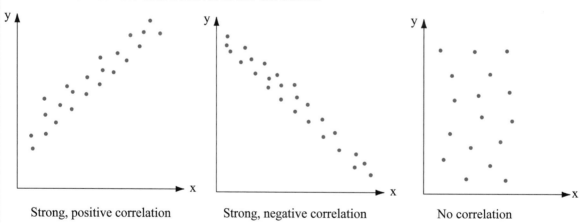

Strong, positive correlation   Strong, negative correlation   No correlation

Example

(a) The table below shows the weight, in kilograms, against the height, in centimetres, of the players in a rugby team.

Weight (kg)	79	85	100	115	89	93	104	105	96	107	115	95	102	107	108
Height (cm)	183	181	187	196	183	184	191	198	193	193	205	190	194	195	198

continued

continued

Solution

Construct a scatter diagram using this data.

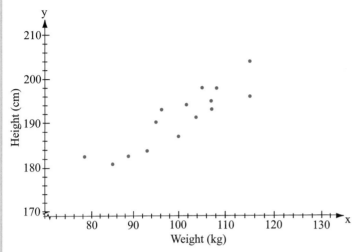

> Look out for

The values on the top of the table are the x-coordinates and those on the bottom are the y-coordinates.

▶ Decide on a scale for each axis. Find the lowest and highest value for each set of data to help you choose the scale. You don't need to start your scale at zero if you put a zigzag line at the start of each axis.

▶ Plot each point with a dot.

▶ Make sure that you plot all the points.

▶ Label each axis.

(b) Draw a line of best fit.

Solution

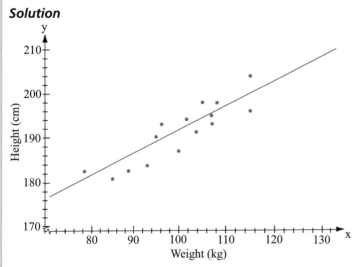

▶ Use the diagram drawn in part (a).

▶ The line of best fit should follow the trend of our data (that is, going from bottom left to top right).

▶ The line should roughly have 50 per cent of the data on either side of it.

continued

continued

(c) Use this line of best fit to estimate the height of a player who weighs 98 kg.

Solution

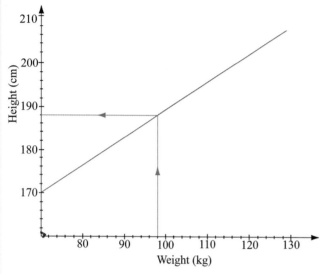

▶ Go straight up from 98 on the x-axis until you hit the line of best fit.
▶ Go straight along until you hit the y-axis.
▶ Read off the height.
▶ Answer the question.

A player who is 98 kg will be approximately 188 centimetres tall.

Example

The scatter diagram below shows the relationship between the Mathematics and Physics scores of a class of pupils.

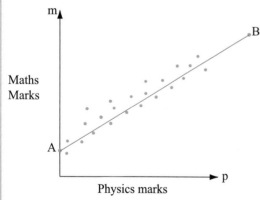

A line of best fit, AB, has been added to the diagram.

Point A represents 0 marks for Physics and 28 marks for Mathematics.
Point B represents 90 marks for Physics and 98 marks for Mathematics.

Find the equation of the straight line AB in terms of p and m.

continued

continued

$(0, 28)$ (x_1, y_1)	▶ A is the point $(0, 28)$.
$(90, 98)$ (x_2, y_2)	▶ B is the point $(90, 98)$.
$m = \dfrac{y_2 - y_1}{x_2 - x_1}$	▶ Find the gradient of the line.
$= \dfrac{98 - 28}{90 - 0}$	
$= \dfrac{7}{9}$	
Cuts y-axis at 28 $\therefore c = 28$	▶ State where the line cuts the y-axis (that is, the y-intercept).
$y = mx + c$	▶ State the formula for a straight line.
$y = \dfrac{7}{9}x + 28$	▶ Substitute the values of m and c into the formula.
$m = \dfrac{7}{9}p + 28$	▶ Write the formula in terms of m and p. Use the diagram to help. The x-axis is labelled p and the y-axis is labelled m.

Standard deviation

$$s = \sqrt{\frac{\Sigma(x - \bar{x})^2}{n-1}} = \sqrt{\frac{\Sigma x^2 - \dfrac{(\Sigma x)^2}{n}}{n-1}}$$

The formulae for standard deviation are given on the formula sheet. Both formulae will give the correct answer.

The range, interquartile range and semi-interquartile range only look at the spread of data between two values. The standard deviation uses all the data. The deviation of a value tells us how much it differs from the mean.

▶ A low standard deviation means that the values in the sample data are close to the mean.

▶ A higher standard deviation means that the values in the sample data are spread out from the mean.

continued

Look out for

The values do not need to be ordered to find the standard deviation.

The $(x - \bar{x})$ column should total zero if you haven't had to round the mean. This is an easy way to see if you have made any mistakes before substituting into the formula.

continued

Example

Alan scored the following percentages in his prelim exams:

63   89   54   68   58   72   65

(a) Calculate the mean and standard deviation of this data.

Solution

x	$(x - \bar{x})$	$(\bar{x} - x)^2$
63	$63 - 67 = -4$	16
89	$89 - 67 = 22$	484
54	$54 - 67 = -13$	169
68	$68 - 67 = 1$	1
58	$58 - 67 = -9$	81
72	$72 - 67 = 5$	25
65	$65 - 67 = -2$	4
469	0	780

$\sum x$ $\sum(x - \bar{x})^2$

$\bar{x} = \dfrac{469}{7} = 67$

▶ Make a table with columns for x, $(x - \bar{x})$ and $(x - \bar{x})^2$.
▶ Fill in the x column and total it.
▶ Find the mean by taking the total of column x and dividing it by 7.
▶ Fill in the $(x - \bar{x})$ column. You can write the part in green if you want but the answer is fine. Totalling this column is optional (see the previous Look Out For).
▶ Fill in the $(x - \bar{x})^2$ column. Remember that a negative number squared gives a positive answer.
▶ Total the $(x - \bar{x})^2$ column.

$s = \sqrt{\dfrac{(x - \bar{x})^2}{n - 1}}$

▶ State the formula.

$= \sqrt{\dfrac{780}{6}}$

▶ Substitute into the formula.

$= \sqrt{130}$

▶ Evaluate the fraction.

$= 11{\cdot}401 \ldots$

▶ Square-root the value.

$= 11{\cdot}4$

▶ Round appropriately.

continued

continued

Alternative Solution

x	x^2
63	3969
89	7921
54	2916
68	4624
58	3364
72	5184
65	4225
469	32203
Σx	Σx^2

▶ Make a table for x and x^2.
▶ Fill in the values for each column and total them.

$$\bar{x} = \frac{\Sigma x}{n} = \frac{469}{7} = 67$$

▶ Use the Σx divided by n to find the mean.

$$s = \sqrt{\frac{\Sigma x^2 - \frac{(\Sigma x)^2}{n}}{n-1}}$$

▶ State the formula.

$$= \sqrt{\frac{32203 - \frac{469^2}{7}}{6}}$$

▶ Substitute into the formula.

$$= \sqrt{\frac{780}{6}}$$

▶ Evaluate the numerator.

$$= \sqrt{130}$$

▶ Evaluate the fraction.

$$= 11\cdot401 \ldots$$

▶ Square-root the value.

$$= 11\cdot4$$

▶ Round appropriately.

Look out for

If using the $\sqrt{\dfrac{\Sigma x^2 - \frac{(\Sigma x)^2}{n}}{n-1}}$ formula, be careful to remember and find the mean if you are asked to do so in the question.

(b) Alan's friend, Liz, sat the same prelim exams and had a mean of 65 and a standard deviation of 8·7.

Make **two** valid comparisons between the friends' results.

Solution

Alan has a higher mean than Liz, so he has, on average, higher results overall.

▶ Make a comparison on the mean. The higher the mean, the higher the overall results.

Liz has a lower standard deviation than Alan, so her results are more consistent.

▶ Make a comparison on the standard deviation. The lower the standard deviation, the less spread there is in the data – that is, the values are closer together.

You need to know how to use the $\sqrt{\dfrac{\sum x^2 - \dfrac{(\sum x)^2}{n}}{n-1}}$ formula, as a question may only give you enough information to use this formula.

Example

The total number of patients who failed to attend their dental appointment each month from July to December last year was recorded.
The data gave the following summary totals:

$$\sum x = 715 \text{ and } \sum x^2 = 85\,875$$

(a) Calculate the mean number of patients per month and standard deviation.

Solution

$$\bar{x} = \frac{\sum x}{n} = \frac{715}{6} = 119\cdot2$$

$$s = \sqrt{\frac{\sum x^2 - \dfrac{(\sum x)^2}{n}}{n-1}}$$

$$= \sqrt{\frac{85875 - \dfrac{715^2}{6}}{5}}$$

$$= \sqrt{\frac{670\cdot833...}{5}}$$

$$= \sqrt{134\cdot166...}$$

$$= 11\cdot583\,...$$

$$= 11\cdot6$$

▶ Use the $\sum x$ divided by n to find the mean.
▶ State the values given. n = 6, the number of months.
▶ There is no choice in this question with the formula you use.

It must be $\sqrt{\dfrac{\sum x^2 - \dfrac{(\sum x)^2}{n}}{n-1}}$

▶ State the formula.
▶ Substitute into the formula.
▶ Evaluate the numerator – don't round it! Use the ANS button on your calculator.
▶ Square-root the value.
▶ Round appropriately.

(b) Another dental surgery records the number of patients per month who failed to attend appointments over the same period of time. The mean was 114·8 and the standard deviation was 12·4. How do the attendance figures compare between the two surgeries?

Solution

Surgery 1 has a higher mean, so, on average, more patients are missing appointments. ▶ Make a comparison of the mean.

Surgery 1 has a lower standard deviation, so the number of patients failing to attend appointments is less varied. ▶ Make a comparison of the standard deviation.

Look out for

Remember to explain what the differences in the mean and standard deviation are in the context of the question.

Probability

The likelihood of an event occurring is called the probability.

$$P(\text{event}) = \frac{\text{number of ways the event can occur}}{\text{total number of outcomes}}$$

Example

On a board game, the number of places moved is decided when two identical dice are rolled simultaneously and the score from each die is added together.

Solution

Find the probability that the total score on adding both numbers is greater than 5 but less than 10.

	1	2	3	4	5	6
1	2	3	4	5	6	7
2	3	4	5	6	7	8
3	4	5	6	7	8	9
4	5	6	7	8	9	10
5	6	7	8	9	10	11
6	7	8	9	10	11	12

$$p(5 < \text{score} < 10) = \frac{20}{36} = \frac{5}{9}$$

continued

▶ We need to consider all the combinations that throwing two dice can give. A table is the best way to work all of these out.

▶ We only have to consider the scores greater than 5 and less than 10. That is : 6, 7, 8 and 9.

▶ You can either fill in the table for every combination or only fill in the results you are looking for (6, 7, 8 or 9).

▶ The number of ways the event can occur is 20.

▶ The total number of outcomes is 36.

▶ State the probability.

▶ Always leave your answer as a fraction in its simplest form.

Example

There are 350 people in the audience at a school dance show. The probability that a person chosen at random from this audience is a school pupil is $\frac{4}{7}$.

How many school pupils are in the audience?

Solution

$350 \div 7 \times 4$

$= 50 \times 4$

$= 200$

There are 200 school pupils in the audience.

▶ Find $\frac{4}{7}$ of 350.

▶ Evaluate the answer.

▶ State your answer.

Glossary

Algebraic fraction   a fraction involving algebraic terms.

Alternate angles   see page 64.

Altitude   the height of an object.

Amplitude   is half the height of a trigonometric function.

Angle of depression   the angle between the horizontal and your line of sight when you look down at an object.

Angle of elevation   the angle between the horizontal and your line of sight when you are looking up at an object.

Annually   means each year.

Appreciation   the increase in value of an item.

Arc   part of the circumference of a circle.

Bisect   Split an angle, line or area equally into two (ie half it).

Boxplot   A type of statistical diagram used to illustrate the five figure summary.

Chord   a straight line going from a point on the circumference to another point on the circumference.

Collinear   a set of points that when plotted make a straight line.

Complementary angles   two or more angles that add together to make 90°.

Compound Interest   interest paid on the full balance of the account including any previous interest earned.

Congruent   when two or more shapes have equal sides and angles.

Conjugate $(x+\sqrt{y})$ is the conjugate of $(x-\sqrt{y})$. When we multiply them together their product is rational (that means it doesn't contain any surds).

Consecutive   following an order, ie 2, 4, 6 are consecutive numbers.

Corresponding angles   see page 64

Cross-section   a 2D shape made by cutting a solid object at 90°. eg a circle is the cross-section of a cylinder, a square is the cross-section of a squared-based pyramid.

Decagon   a 10 sided polygon.

Denominator   the bottom line of a fraction.

Depreciation   the increase in value of an item.

Direct Variation   see page 12.

Dotplot   a statistical diagram similar to a bar graph but dots are used instead of columns to display the data.

Equation   a statement showing 2 expressions that are equal to each other

Equilateral   a triangle with 3 equal sides, 3 equal angles and 3 lines of symmetry.

Evaluate   find out the answer.

Expression   a collection of algebraic terms.

Factor   a term which divides exactly into another term.

Factorise   to separate into factors

Five figure summary   stating the lowest, highest, median, lower quartile and upper quartile for a set of data.

Formula   an algebraic statement that allows you to work out something by substituting values into an equation.

Function   is a way of describing how 2 variables are related. A function can be used to name a graph.

Gradient   the steepness of a line (vertical ÷ horizontal).

Hexagon   a 6 sided polygon.

Index   a power. The plural of index is indices.

Inequality   when a quantity is 'greater than', 'greater than or equal to', 'less than' or 'less than or equal to' the other quantity. ie the two quantities are never equal to each other.

Integer   a positive or negative whole number.

Interquartile range   the difference between the lower quartile and the upper quartile.

Intersect   to cross at a point.

Inverse   the opposite or reverse, eg multiply is the inverse of divide.

Inverse Variation   see page 13.

Irrational number   a number that can't be written as a fraction when the numerator and denominator are integers. eg π, $\sqrt{3}$

Isosceles   a triangle with 2 equal sides, 2 equal angles and 1 line of symmetry.

Joint variation   see page 14.

Linear equation   an equation containing terms where the highest power is 1.

Linear expression   an expression containing terms where the highest power is 1.

Linear graph   a straight line graph ($y=mx+c$).

Median   the middle value in an ordered set of data.

Multiple   all the numbers created by multiplying one number by another number eg 15, 20 and 25 are multiples of 5.

Non-zero   not equal to zero.

Numerator   the top line of a fraction.

Octagon   an 8 sided polygon.

Origin   the point (0, 0).

Parabola   the graph of a quadratic equation.

Pentagon   a 5 sided polygon.

Per annum   each year (annually).

Period   the number of degrees in which a trigonometric graph occurs.

Perpendicular bisector   is a line which cuts another line in half at 90°.

Perpendicular   is a line at a right angle to another line.

Polygon   a 2D shape of many sides.

Power   the number of times a number is multiplied by itself eg 4^3 is 4×4×4 and the power is 3.

Prime number   a number which has only 2 factors, itself and 1, eg 2, 3, 5, 7, 11,…

Prism   a 3D shape with a uniform cross-section.

Probability   the chance of an event occurring. It can be written as a fraction, decimal or percentage.

Product   the answer when 2 or more numbers are multiplied together.

Quadratic equation   an equation containing terms where the highest power is 2. It has 2 solutions. (Also known as a trinomial).

Quadratic expression   an expression containing terms where the highest power is 2.

Quadrilateral   a four sided polygon such as a square, rectangle, kite, parallelogram, kite, trapezium or rhombus.

Quartiles   one of three values which split ordered data into four intervals. The lower quartile is a quarter-way, the median halfway and the upper quartile three quarters-way.

Glossary

Quotient   the result of dividing one number by another number eg 6 is the quotient of 30÷5.

Range   the highest value subtracted the lowest value in an ordered set of data.

Ratio   a comparison of part-to-part.

Rational denominator   a denominator that does not contain any surds.

Rational number   a number which can be written as a fraction where the numerator and denominator are both integers.

Real number   the set of rational and irrational numbers.

Reciprocal   the inverse of a fraction, eg $\frac{3}{2}$ is the reciprocal of $\frac{2}{3}$.

Regular   a shape with equal sides.

Root of an equation   the values where a graph cuts the x-axis.

Scale factor   the multiplier used to enlarge or reduce a shape.

Scalene   a triangle with no equal sides, no equal angles and no lines of symmetry.

Scientific Notation   a way of writing large or small numbers in the form $a \times 10^n$ where a is a number between 1 and 10 (but never is 10) and n is an integer.

Sector   a section of a circle formed between 2 radii and an arc.

Segment   a section of a circle formed by a chord and an arc.

Semi-interquartile range   half the interquartile range.

Sequence   a collection of terms following a pattern or rule.

Significant Figure   the number of digits in a number to give a certain degree of accuracy.

Similar   Shapes are mathematically similar if one is a scaled version of the other.

Simple Interest   interest paid only on the initial amount of money and not on previous interest earned.

Simplify   to make it easier to understand.

Simultaneous equation   two linear equations which can be solved to find 2 unknown values.

Standard deviation   the measure of spread of a set of data.

Stem-and-leaf   a statistical diagram that displays an ordered set of data.

Subject (of a formula)   the letter that equals the rest of the formula is the subject. V is the subject in $V = lbh$.

Substitute   replacing a letter with a number (or another letter).

Sum   the total when adding two or more values together.

Supplementary angles   two or more angles adding together to make 180°.

Surd   the root of a number that cannot be worked out exactly eg $\sqrt{10}$, $\sqrt[3]{20}$.

Surface area   the area of each surface of a 3D shape added together.

Tangent to a circle   a straight line which touches the circle at only one point on the circumference and makes a right angle with the radius of the circle.

Term   part of an expression, equation or sequence eg $2x$ is a term of the equation $x^2 + 2x - 5 = 0$.

Trigonometric function   a function involving sine, cosine or tangent.

Trinomial   see quadratic equation.

Uniform cross-section   the area of the cross-sectional shape is exactly the same size throughout the solid shape.

Variable   takes a range of values eg on $y = 2x + 1x$ and y are variables

Vertically opposite angles   See page 64

94